PENGUIN BOOKS

THE PLUNDERED PLANET

Paul Collier is Professor of Economics and Director of the Centre for the Study of African Economies at Oxford University and a former director of Development Research at the World Bank. In addition to the award-winning *The Bottom Billion*, he is the author of *Wars, Guns, and Votes: Democracy in Dangerous Places*.

PAUL COLLIER

The Plundered Planet

How to Reconcile
Prosperity with Nature

PENGUIN BOOKS

PENGUIN BOOKS

Published by the Penguin Group
Penguin Books Ltd, 80 Strand, London WC2R 0RL, England
Penguin Group (USA) Inc., 375 Hudson Street, New York, New York 10014, USA
Penguin Group (Canada), 90 Eglinton Avenue East, Suite 700, Toronto, Ontario, Canada M4P 2Y3
(a division of Pearson Penguin Canada Inc.)
Penguin Ireland, 25 St Stephen's Green, Dublin 2, Ireland (a division of Penguin Books Ltd)
Penguin Group (Australia), 250 Camberwell Road, Camberwell, Victoria 3124, Australia
(a division of Pearson Australia Group Pty Ltd)
Penguin Books India Pvt Ltd, 11 Community Centre,
Panchsheel Park, New Delhi – 110 017, India
Penguin Group (NZ), 67 Apollo Drive, Rosedale, Auckland 0632, New Zealand
(a division of Pearson New Zealand Ltd)
Penguin Books (South Africa) (Pty) Ltd, 24 Sturdee Avenue,
Rosebank, Johannesburg 2196, South Africa

Penguin Books Ltd, Registered Offices: 80 Strand, London WC2R 0RL, England

www.penguin.com

First published in the United States of America by Oxford University Press 2010
First published in Great Britain by Allen Lane 2010
Published in Penguin Books 2011
005

Copyright © Paul Collier, 2010

ISBN: 978-0-1410-4214-5

www.greenpenguin.co.uk

For Stephanie (aged one) and Alexander (aged three),
who will inherit the natural assets and liabilities that
we bequeath, and who already know a thing or two about
natural disorder.

Contents

Preface

I GREW UP BEFORE NATURE WAS DISCOVERED. Today, our mismanagement of the natural world is widely recognized. It fills blogs and packs conferences, and "environmental studies" sits high and proud in the school curriculum. But when I was at school it was called "nature study," and we slept through it. At college, while others were waking up to disorder in the natural world, I woke up to global poverty and the tragedy of frustrated lives. My parents had lacked the opportunities that had opened for me. I saw in global poverty that same lack of opportunity writ large.

Environmentalism looked like the indulgence of people who took their prosperity for granted. Restoring environmental order and eradicating global poverty have become the two defining challenges of our era. Each has its adherents, often opposed. A number of environmentalists in the developed world are wary of the spread of global prosperity, arguing that it would wreck the planet. Conversely, in the poorer countries of the world—the bottom billion—many people are wary of environmentalism, seeing it as an attempt by the richer countries to haul up the ladder. Belatedly, I have accepted the importance of nature. This book reflects my own struggle to reconcile the quest for global prosperity with an ethical approach to the natural world. As Nicholas Stern argues, if we fail in either challenge, we fail in both. If we permit natural disorder to continue, it will indeed frustrate the eradication of global poverty. Yet if part of the world continues to be marginalized, it will frustrate the cooperation on which the restoration of natural order depends. The two goals are linked by something even more powerful than this threat of shared failure. Nature is the key asset of the poorest countries: managed responsibly it will power their ascent to prosperity. Yet the scramble for prosperity is driving the plunder of nature. Natural order—the responsible management of nature—can deliver prosperity, but prosperity alone cannot deliver natural order.

The tension between prosperity and plunder is now apparent. The world's voracious demand for raw materials has driven up the prices of natural resources and food to unprecedented levels; it took a global financial crisis to puncture them. In turn, the price hike has triggered a new scramble for Africa, pumping revenues into the continent. China, the giant of the emerging market economies, comes without the baggage of colonialism; indeed, many of the countries of the bottom billion have long regarded it as an ally. But from the perspective of the rich countries, the Chinese arrival in Africa is not just unwelcome competition. It threatens to undermine international efforts to reform the governance of the extractive industries, after decades of corruption and exploitation. The Chinese president has toured Africa with the message "we won't ask any questions." Is China finally freeing the bottom billion from the lingering embrace of colonialism or plunging them back into a shameful past?

While abroad the emerging market economies buy up resources, at home their industries emit carbon dioxide. For the next twenty years China plans to construct more power stations annually than the entire British stock. The carbon threatens to overheat the planet. Yet the threat has become a money-spinner. Under the new *Clean Development Mechanism* Chinese companies are paid what looks disturbingly like protection money for not emitting even more. But from the perspective of the emerging market economies the belated concern about pollution of the richest societies is hypocrisy: they are merely doing what the rich countries have already done. If the rich want them to behave differently, the rich must bear the cost.

In rich societies intensifying scarcities of natural resources and a deteriorating climate have conjured up a sense of Armageddon. For the romantics, those who believe we must radically alter our relationship to nature and scale back consumption, this is music: global industrial capitalism is finally getting its comeuppance, drowning in its own contradictions. From Prince Charles to street protesters they advocate a future in which mankind returns to harmony with nature. The lifestyle of the future will be organic, holistic, self-sufficient, local, and small-scale. Not only should we completely amend our lifestyle, we will beat our breasts: paying compensation to the rest of the world for having despoiled nature and overheated the planet.

Juxtaposed against the romantics are the ostriches. If there is to be a scramble for natural resources the important thing is to win it. Fussing about governance will hand contracts to the Chinese. Limiting our carbon emissions unnecessarily threatens our lifestyle. The climate might not deteriorate, and anyway the future can be left to take care of itself. The romantics and the ostriches are each half right.

The romantics are right that we are seriously mismanaging nature and that our practices are indefensible. The ostriches are right that much of what is said about nature is ridiculously pious, casting the rich countries as villains and the rest of the world as their victims. Such self-flagellation is unwarranted and counterproductive, relegating societies that will need to be essential participants in solutions to the role of passive recipients of our largesse.

But the romantics and the ostriches are also each half wrong. Both the romantics and the ostriches will take us to oblivion, albeit by different routes. Run by the romantics, the world would starve; run by the ostriches, it would burn. The romantics are a serious menace to global agriculture. The ostriches are complicit in the plunder of natural assets. Decisions must be founded on a proper sense of responsibility toward both the global poor and the future, not blinkered self-interest. In short, *The Plundered Planet* is written for people who are neither filled with a saintly loathing of modernity nor are ethically blocks of stone: people who have, perhaps, grown a little impatient with the profusion of homilies about our duty to sustain the natural world in the condition to which it has become accustomed, but who nonetheless recognize that a cheery disregard for nature would be whistling in the dark.

Nature matters and we are making a mess of it. This matters most for the people who live in the world's poorest countries. For them the situation poses both an opportunity and a threat of vital proportions. My theme is not how the natural world can be preserved as an end in itself, but how it can be harnessed to transform these poor societies without placing unreasonable demands on the rest of us. My lodestar for what is reasonable to expect of us is the combination of compassion and self-interest that, I believe, is how most of us try to conduct our lives.

The opportunity that nature presents to the countries of the bottom billion is the enormous value of their natural assets. During the commodity bonanza of 2005–8 around $1 trillion was extracted from their territories in oil alone. The pulse of new money could have financed their transformation. The bonanza was a repeat on a grander scale of the boom of the 1970s. As many are now all too painfully aware, that had been a missed opportunity during which the revenues from the exploitation of natural assets were plundered, some by foreign companies, some by corrupt politicians, and some because of popular short-sightedness. Sometimes plunder turned destructive, turning opportunity into catastrophe. As I will show, even the bonanza of 2005–8 is but a shadow of the potential revenues. The key question is whether enough has changed to prevent these funds from being dissipated.

While being a huge opportunity, the commodity boom of 2005–8 was a two-edged sword. The price hike in basic foods hit some of the most vulnerable people on earth. Slum dwellers in the big coastal cities bought their food at prices set on the world market. Even before the price hike, with half their budget devoted to food, such households had been barely staying afloat. Over the centuries hungry slum dwellers have been the stuff of political protest. As prices rose capital cities were ravaged by riots, sometimes toppling governments as in Haiti. Global agriculture had failed to keep abreast of global demand.

Exacerbating the food shortages is climate change. For the bottom billion this is not a slow burn: they are in the forefront of overheating. Already too hot, most models predict that their climates will deteriorate more rapidly and more substantially than those in other regions. In Africa, the core of the bottom billion, the climate is already deteriorating. Its countries are doubly exposed: not only do they face the greatest climate degradation, their agriculture-dominated economies are far more sensitive to climate than the industrial and service economies of richer countries.

Yet this presents the countries of the bottom billion with a potential opportunity. Climate change is driven by the uncontrolled accumulation of a natural liability: carbon dioxide. Due to their poverty they emit little carbon: as part of a global deal they could acquire emission rights equal to the past emissions of the rich countries. The sale of carbon rights would become a new natural asset.

Potentially, the opportunities far outweigh the threats. The threats from nature are not intrinsic; they arise because many natural assets are peculiarly exposed to plunder. Plunder is an economic phenomenon: if incentives are misaligned natural assets are depleted and natural liabilities accumulated, without due regard to the future. But if economic behavior can be understood it can be changed.

In an ideal world, the main centers of research on the problems of the bottom billion would be located within their own societies. But in an ideal world there would be no bottom billion. The poverty of these societies has condemned their universities to struggle at the margins of the international research community, their brightest scholars poached by richer institutions elsewhere. Instead, serious research on the poorest societies, and how best nature can be turned to their advantage, is clustered within a few research universities in North America and Europe.

Oxford is one of those centers, attracting scholars from around the world. My own team of young researchers provides an example, and this book is largely built on the back of their work: Stefan Dercon, who is Belgian; Benedikt Goderis, who is Dutch; Anke Hoeffer, who is German; Victor Davies, who is Sierra Leonean; Lisa Chauvet and Marguerite Duponchel, who are French; and Chris Adam, who, like me, is British. But much of the heavy intellectual lifting has been done by my colleague Tony Venables: there is scarcely an idea in this book that has not been either jointly forged or argued out between us. While Tony is complicit in the ideas, the errors of execution are authentically my own. I have tried to translate those ideas from the precise but opaque format of modern economic research into something that can be read beyond a narrow circle of professionals.

Writing a book needs a time of quiet. The unexpected arrival of Alex and Stephanie brought a joyful natural disorder into our lives. From within this disorder my wife, Pauline, carved out a little fortress within which *The Plundered Planet* could take shape. She is an environmental historian and so I have plundered her ideas as well. Indeed, our marriage might be a metaphor for the larger theme of this book: how environmentalists and economists can benefit from alliance.

The Ethics of Nature

PART 1

The Ethics of Nature

CHAPTER 1

Poverty and Plunder

THE BOTTOM BILLION HAS MISSED OUT on global prosperity. The current reality for these people is poverty; the issue is whether this will also be the fate of their children. The path that the rest of the world took to lift itself out of poverty—industrialization—is proving much more difficult for these latecomers. Industry has globalized, and China's combination of huge scale with low wages makes it hyper-competitive when pitched against new entrants. Farming offers them little promise. In Africa, home to most of the bottom billion, agricultural productivity has already fallen far behind international standards. Global warming is likely to widen the gulf, making Africa even hotter and drier, while warming the vast tracts of North America and Eurasia that are currently too cold for cultivation. Nor is aid likely to rescue them; it is under increasing attack, sometimes for good reason, and is being squeezed by the need to rein in fiscal deficits.

The countries of the bottom billion have one lifeline: nature. Nature has the potential to lift most of them to prosperity. But nature does not come on a platter. Mankind was not born into an Eden, but into a harsh environment in which we struggled to survive even in tiny numbers. Gradually the natural world has become more valuable to mankind as technology has progressed. Technology turns nature into an asset. However, technology alone merely gives those assets the potential to be valuable to society. Natural assets have no natural owners, and as they become valuable they can trigger a struggle for possession in which their value is dissipated in the costs of struggle. Prehistory was violent; some anthropologists estimate that around 40 percent of deaths were due to fighting. As technical discoveries conferred value on rare natural phenomena such as flint, disputed ownership was inevitable. Basic economics tells us that the value of the effort put into getting possession of natural assets would escalate until it was approximately equal to the value of the assets to be acquired. Modern versions of the struggle are usually less violent, although they can harness means for killing far beyond those available in the Stone Age. But even when nonviolent, the same basic economics applies to these struggles: they can be hugely costly to the country with the assets. If resource-extraction companies routinely bribe its ministers for the rights to exploit their nature, political power becomes so valuable that everything is bent to the purpose of its acquisition. Public spending turns into patronage, laws and courts become instruments of reward for supporters and punishment for opponents.

Technology turns nature into assets, yet their value to society is only potential. For natural assets actually to be valuable instead of being dissipated in competitive struggle, their ownership must be regulated. The challenge of harnessing nature can be summarized in a simple formula, a formula that the world as a whole, and the poorest countries in particular, must master: *nature + technology + regulation = prosperity*.

In the societies of the bottom billion that equation has usually not been achieved even as technology has continued to confer value on more and more natural phenomena in their territory. Coltan, of which the Democratic Republic of the Congo has a huge endowment, became valuable as a result of the invention of the mobile phone, for which it is an essential ingredient. Advances in copper refining enabled ores in Zambia that once would have been left as uneconomic to be mined profitably. But technology is a fickle friend: it can take away value as well as add it. Nitrates and guano dung were the oil of the nineteenth century; technology has now developed substitutes, as it will for oil. And technology can turn nature nasty: the technology that has given us cheap energy has also given us carbon dioxide that will overheat the planet.

While the fickleness of technology can be a problem, the key failures have been due to the lack of regulation. Around the world people are now much more aware of the need for regulation as a result of the global crisis, brought on by poor regulation of financial markets. The origin of that inadequacy was hostility to regulation among economists that extended far beyond the financial markets: we had all become over-enthused by the magic of the market. When I was newly brought in to the World Bank by Joe Stiglitz to direct its research department, I remember listening to a seminar presentation on why there should be no regulatory safety standards in fairgrounds. The profession is grudgingly realizing that its ideological opposition to regulation was overdone. Without regulation the potential of natural assets cannot be realized, and natural liabilities such as carbon dioxide can become so dangerous as to justify, for once, that hackneyed term "weapons of mass destruction."

Regulation requires good governance. The planet's natural assets are mostly on and under land controlled by the world's 194 governments, which vary greatly in their competence and their accountability to citizens. A convenient way of thinking about the planet's land area is to group it into four equal quadrants. The developed countries in that wealthy club, the Organisation for Economic Co-operation and Development, account for 80 percent of the world economy. However, they control only one of the land quadrants. At the other end of the spectrum, the countries that have missed out on development—the bottom billion—account for merely 1 percent of the world economy, yet they, too, also have one of the land quadrants. The third quadrant belongs to Russia and China and their satellites. The final quadrant is everyone else: essentially, the emerging market economies. In each of these political arenas, global natural order depends upon the incentives for plunder being countered by effective regulation.

Regulation requires good governance, but most of the societies of the bottom billion have had weak governance. The consequence might be summarized in another simple formula: *nature + technology – regulation = plunder*. Plunder has dominated the history of the exploitation of natural assets in the poorest societies. What should have been the lifeline by which these societies haul themselves out of poverty, has instead produced wasted opportunity. Although basic economics suggests that the value of natural assets is dissipated by an equally costly struggle over possession, more sophisticated analysis shows that the outcome of that struggle can be even worse. Basic economics just predicts its cost to the participants, but not to bystanders. Because of this potential for harm the discovery of natural assets can turn into a curse. While the societies of the bottom billion have been the most vulnerable to plunder, even middle-income countries have been put at risk. Ernesto Zedillo, the former president of Mexico, views current Mexican society as a tragedy for which oil is responsible. It has dragged the society down when it could have lifted the economy up.

The poor governance of natural assets also happens in the wealthy countries of the OECD. At the national level governance of natural assets is usually satisfactory, but this stops at the border. Sometimes nature does not respect frontiers. For those natural assets and liabilities that are global, such as the fish of the oceans and the carbon of the skies, plunder is currently the standard. Indeed the most energetic plunderers of these global natural assets are the companies and citizens of the rich societies. Regulation is necessary, yet most economists are doubtful. Their suspicion is not unjustified: rules are not set by Platonic Guardians wisely guiding our societies; they are set by the balances of political pressures. A well-functioning democracy will formulate the rules that most people want, but what people want depends upon what they understand. I wrote *The Bottom Billion* because I recognized that until citizens were better informed about the distinctive problems of the poorest countries democratic governments would adopt "gesture politics." Policies that looked good in the headlines were preferred to more effective policies too sophisticated to be appreciated. In a democracy, regulation of the natural world can be no better than popular understanding of why it is needed and the rules that govern nature will reflect any misunderstandings.

In the rich countries, where decades of unprecedented economic growth have induced rapid social change and religious belief has waned, nature has become the last constant. It is seen as under siege, threatened by the march of scientific technology. The "birth of the modern" is commonly dated to the end of the Napoleonic Wars in 1815. It was not long before nature was being enlisted into the diagnosis of the discontentment of civilization. By 1821 the French-German Enlightenment philosopher Baron d'Holbach was writing, "Man is only unhappy because he does not understand nature." If only we could get back to nature we could get off the psychiatrist's couch.The more prosperity has distanced us from nature, the more we have demanded that governments protect it from science. And the more emotive the issue involved the more it is apparent, as with stem-cell research and genetically modified food.

Agriculture, as the economic activity that most directly impinges on nature, has borne the brunt of these sentiments. But the mis-understandings of ordinary citizens offer fertile opportunities for special interests. Regulation not only protects, it redistrib-utes. Regulations can be manipulated by interest groups to their advantage and in the rich countries the agricultural lobby has thrived on popular misunderstandings which, through our aid programs, have extended to Africa. With their organic cultivation practices, production for self-sufficiency, and family organiza-tion, small farmers in developing countries are perceived as the last bastion of the pretechnological, precommercial, preindustrial lifestyle, a "peasant" lifestyle that needs to be preserved. As the peasant and industrial lifestyles have further diverged, reflecting the growth of our economies and the stagnation of theirs, the peasant lifestyle has come to emblemize a harmonious life. The development NGOs, dedicated as they are to the eradication of poverty, also reflect the environmental concerns of the wealthy countries that fund them. Their attitude to a local farming econ-omy can therefore border on the schizophrenic: they want both change and preservation.

The victims of today's curtailment of stem-cell research are tomor-row's incurables. But the victims of the anti-science, pro-peasant regulation of agriculture are today's poor. Curtailing technology and discouraging the commercialization of African agriculture have tended to increase the price of food, and food is the main item of expenditure for poor households. Here's a final formula: *nature + regulation − technology = hunger*.

Environmentalists versus Economists?

Environmentalists and economists have been cat and dog. Environmentalists see economists as the mercenaries of a culture of greed, the cheerleaders of an affluence that is unsustainable. Economists see environmentalists as romantic reactionaries, wanting to apply the brakes to an economic engine that is at last reducing global poverty.

The argument of this book is that environmentalists and economists need each other. They need each other because they are on the same side in a war that is being lost. The natural world is being plundered: natural assets are being depleted and natural liabilities accumulated in a manner that both environmentalists and economists would judge to be unethical. But the need for an alliance runs deeper than the practical necessities of preventing defeat. Environmentalists and economists need each other intellectually.

In 2009 Sir Partha Dasgupta, an economist at Cambridge, comprehensively reviewed how the profession has analyzed the natural world. His conclusion was that it "remains isolated from the main body of contemporary economic thinking." Even when economists incorporate nature, they treat it as they do any other asset: natural capital is simply part of the capital stock, to be exploited for the benefit of mankind.

Since the *Stern Review of the Economics of Climate Change* of 2006 one aspect of the natural world—that it is warming—has suddenly slammed into the economic mainstream. Lord Stern commanded sufficient respect to force the profession to pay attention to the costs of global warming and the options for mitigation. The result has been an acrimonious battle among economists as different models have produced widely differing results. Yet as Stern has stressed, the key issues are not technical, they are ethical. Policy choices should turn on the responsibilities of the present generation to the future. Yet mainstream economics has blundered into climate change guided only by an ethical framework that is simply inadequate to deal with nature because it ignores rights. Rights are central to the ethics of the natural world: the rights of the present versus the future, and my rights versus yours. Environmentalists bring a fundamental insight that economists have missed. Nature is *special*: our rights over the natural world are not the same as our rights over the man-made world. Economists need that insight in rethinking the ethical assumptions made in their models.

It will come as no surprise to most people that economists need an injection of ethics. Survey evidence finds that economics students tend to be more self-interested than other students. Either economics attracts the selfish, or worse, it inculcates greed. Economists indeed assume that people are interested only in their own consumption, yet paradoxically, economists judge the world according to an ethical framework that is selfless in the extreme: Utilitarianism. As adopted by economists, Utilitarianism is an austere, universal value system that is impossibly demanding; according to its judgments even noneconomists are selfish. Given the gulf between the values economists use to judge the world and the values they assume ordinary people to hold, many economists conclude that ordinary people cannot be trusted adequately to protect the interests of the future: they are ostriches. Economists share Plato's view that the ideal government would be composed of wise Guardians, although, of course, those Guardians should be economists rather than philosophers. In advocating an override of democracy, economists dig themselves deeper into ethical trouble. Nor is their approach realistic: government priorities will inevitably reflect the preferences of their citizens.

Yet in this, too, economists can learn much from environmentalists. One of the founding texts of modern environmentalism is *Our Plundered Planet*, by Fairfield Osborn. Originally published in 1948, Osborn—who was then the president of the New York Zoological Society—sought to awaken ordinary citizens to the unsustainable exploitation of nature.

The Plundered Planet proposes a synthesis in the practical value systems used by environmentalists and economists. Environmentalists are right that each generation has responsibilities for natural assets that it does not have toward other assets. But economists are right that nature is an asset, to be used for the benefit of mankind. We are not *curators* of the natural world, preserving nature as an end in itself. We are not ethically obliged to preserve every tiger, or every tree. We are *custodians* of the value of natural assets. We are ethically obliged to pass on to future generations the equivalent value of the natural assets that we were bequeathed by the past. The natural world indeed presents us with distinct obligations, but those obligations are essentially economic.

In the proposed alliance between environmentalists and economists the common enemies are the ostriches and the romantics. The ostriches will plunder the natural world. Sometimes plunder takes a form that is instantly recognizable as unethical. But more often the true consequences of an apparently legitimate action have to be teased out from a chain of decisions. As a result, plunder goes largely unrecognized. In the countries of the bottom billion there is a complex chain of decisions the end result of which is that natural assets are being extracted without sustainable benefit to ordinary citizens. In the rich countries activities that until recently were innocuous, now accumulate natural liabilities. In each case, the culprits are largely unaware of their culpability. The romantics will leave the potential of the natural world untapped; preserved rather than harnessed. The lifeline for the bottom billion will not be seized.

The poorest countries need rapid economic growth and this creates a potential tension between poverty reduction and the preservation of nature. Environmentalists have been right to stress that economic development must be sustainable, but economists bring the insight that sustainability need not imply preservation. If environmentalists insist on the preservation of each aspect of the natural world they are liable to find themselves on the wrong side in the struggle against global poverty.

Plunder and romanticism are so rife precisely because ordinary citizens are insufficiently informed about the opportunities and threats that nature poses to have forced governments into effective regulation. In the task of building an informed citizenry the starting point is an ethics of nature that people in societies with widely different value systems can understand and accept. Neither the romantic variant of environmentalism that sees nature as an end in itself, nor the austere universalism of economic Utilitarianism, can provide such a foundation. The most difficult wars to win are those that must be fought on two fronts. It is more straightforward, psychologically more satisfying and dramatic to have only a single enemy. Views can be aligned on a continuum, with the good and the true at one end and the bad and the wrong at the other. The romantics among environmentalists and the Utilitarian Platonic Guardians among economists see nature as a single-front war. The romantics regard economic growth as the enemy; the Platonic Guardians regard the values of ordinary citizens as the enemy. But most struggles in development are not like that: sanity lies in the middle rather than at the extremes. Aid provides an example. It is neither a panacea nor a menace.

In this book I am going to try to turn the exploitation of nature and its assets into a two-front war, expanding what is currently no-man's land into a place where all but the romantics and the ostriches can feel at home. The romantics and the ostriches each tap into a range of emotions: the romantics on guilt, fear and nostalgia; the ostriches on greed and optimism. But the devil need not have all the best tunes: effective solutions to vital problems that have been intractable lay where they always have—in the center.

CHAPTER 2

Is Nature Priceless?

THE INDIGNANT TEARS OF A CHILD command attention. Daniel, aged eight, has just learned about the Brazilian rain forest and it has moved him to his first expression of political outrage. It is directed at me, not as his father, but as representative of the generation of adults who are destroying something precious before he reaches the age at which he can stop us. Through sobs and rage he shouts, "Tell the president!" Having seen me on television, Daniel has a somewhat inflated impression of my influence. Eight-year-olds are not, on the whole, always repositories of good sense, and Daniel is no exception. But by chance his anger is right on target: son and father are ethically aligned in the battleground of natural assets.

First, the left flank. I agree with environmentalists that nature is special: at some level most of us recognize that. But why is it special? Mainstream environmentalists, such as Stewart Brand, offer one answer. Nature is especially vulnerable and that matters because, being dependent upon it, mankind is thereby vulnerable. But as

Brand argues, many environmentalists are carrying ideological baggage that needs to be discarded. For romantic environmentalists nature is incommensurate with the mundane business of the economy: it is in some way ethically prior. Echoing Baron d'Holbach's diagnosis of modern angst, they see industrial capitalism as having divorced us from the natural world which it is rapidly destroying. You can sense their discomfort with modern industrial society in the language that they use, replete with words such as "organic" and "holistic." For a recent variation on the theme of Holbach, watch Prince Charles delivering the BBC's 2009 distinguished Dimbleby Lecture.

Perhaps man needs to return to a simpler, nonindustrial lifestyle. Prince Charles produces organic food, and he has created a village, Poundsbury, in the style of the eighteenth century—the last age prior to industrialization. At the extreme end of romantic environmentalism the diagnosis is more radical: mankind itself has become the enemy of what is truly good. Reflecting these sentiments, there is now a considerable cult that relishes the prospect of the extinction of mankind. Only then can nature be restored. Portrayals of earth after man attract huge audiences. The romantic wing of environmentalists appears prepared to sacrifice industrial society in order to *preserve* nature; the extreme appears willing to sacrifice the human race.

Who Owns Nature?

I doubt whether Daniel is a romantic environmentalist. The source of his outrage cannot plausibly be traced to his being ill-at-ease with modern industrial society. I wish he were a little less at ease with it, for the detritus is littered all around his room. Of course, he was worried about the rain forest because it is irreplaceable. But he was angry because he felt that his rights of ownership were being infringed. Children have a keen sense of property ownership; they know what is theirs and they usually want to keep it that way. But why does Daniel feel that he has rights over the Brazilian rain forest? After all he has never even seen it. He makes no such claim on our neighbor's new car, which he sees every day and which contrasts so unfortunately with our own battered specimen. It is because the Brazilian rain forest is a special sort of asset: a natural asset. What is special about natural assets is their ownership. *Natural assets have no natural owners.* This proposition has far-reaching implications, such as for thinking about climate change. But first and foremost it places government at the center of the action.

All rights of ownership over assets are social constructs, but with man-made assets the initial rights of ownership follow directly from their making: the firm which makes the car initially owns it, although they can then sell it to me. Of course, since all property rights are social constructs we can and do set limits to ownership. Although the firm that builds a vehicle owns the vehicle, if it sells it at a profit then some of that profit belongs to the government. The idea that the creation of an asset should confer rights of ownership makes a lot of sense both ethically and practically. Ethically, the creator has expended effort and value in creating the asset. Practically, if newly created assets were to be promptly confiscated by others, there would be no incentive to creating them. For these reasons vesting initial ownership rights in the creator of the asset is supported virtually across the political spectrum, with the exception of primitive communists.

So much for created assets. Natural assets are different. By definition, they are not man-made. Some people think that they were created by God, others by chance. Either way, their process of creation did not give any steer as to who should own them.

Recalling that natural substances only acquire value as a result of technological discoveries, should the discoverers of the technology have a claim on the resulting natural assets? Should Nokia, for example, the Finnish company that pioneered the mobile phone, be given the rights over African coltan? Should the world's automobile manufacturers own the world's oil? It hardly sounds like a reasonable ethical rallying cry. Natural assets simply do not have any natural owners and so societies are free to assign the rights any way they like. The process by which ownership rights over natural assets are acquired has potent economic implications both for the distribution of income, and for efficiency. Imagine a society in which government is absent. No authority would be able to construct and enforce property rights over natural assets.

In this society physical control of the asset is all that matters. This gives rise to three problems: mal-distribution, rent-seeking, and uncertainty. Mal-distribution comes about partly because the strong are advantaged over the weak, but it is compounded by chance: some territories are better endowed than others. If we imagine the population distinguished in the two dimensions of strength and luck, the natural assets are acquired disproportionately by those who are lucky and strong. "Rent-seeking" is the technical term for ways, including violence, to acquire ownership. Basic economics predicts that the value of natural assets, which technically are unearned "rents," will be matched by the efforts to "seek" those rents, so that the potential social value of natural assets will be dissipated by the costs incurred. In the absence of effective rules there will inevitably be uncertainty as to whether current control over a natural asset can be maintained. With control perceived as temporary, the private incentive is to deplete assets quickly even if this is socially more costly than necessary. As a result, those natural assets that are easy to find will rapidly be plundered. Americans know this only too well: once the West started to be settled even at very low population densities, the immense herds of buffalo were rapidly hunted to the verge of extinction.

I saw another instance of plunder in 2008 as I clattered over the landscape of Hispaniola in a Russian helicopter. Hispaniola is the name that Columbus gave to the first island he discovered in the Americas. It is now divided down the middle into two countries, the Dominican Republic and Haiti. Whereas the Dominican Republic has been well-governed, Haiti has long been synonymous with weak and corrupt governance. Indeed, in rural areas the government presence is still minimal. The North coast of Haiti, over which I was flying, is a favored destination for cruise ships, but many tourists do not even realize that they are landing there: in the brochures it is still described as Hispaniola. I was there because Ban Ki-Moon, Secretary-General of the United Nations, had read *The Bottom Billion*. Recognizing that Haiti had many of the problems I had tried to analyze, he had sent me there in the hope that I might be of some use. Haiti once had a natural asset—its forest cover. But no longer. Flying over the landscape, I could see bare hills spread out beneath me; bare hills, more bare hills, and then quite abruptly, trees, trees, and more trees. The helicopter had crossed the border with the Dominican Republic. On the Haitian side of the border there is 2 percent tree cover, on the other side, 37 percent. Hispaniola is not a big island, and the explanation was not due to climate. Indeed, in the 1920s over 60 percent of Haiti had been covered in trees. The key difference was in governance: in the absence of secure property rights the trees of Haiti had been plundered.

Buffalos and trees are vulnerable because they are highly visible. Natural assets that are hidden suffer the opposite fate: they are ignored. Because discoveries cannot be protected there is no incentive to undertake search. It is more efficient to wait for others to find natural assets and then wrest control away from them through superior strength. Hence, they remain undiscovered. In fact, since the process of losing control of a natural asset that you have found beneath where you live is likely to be nasty, there is even an incentive to avoid noticing what might be there.

Valuable natural assets, such as oil and metal ores, lie hidden beneath the ground until they are discovered. The term for them is "subsoil assets." In 2000 a global inventory of subsoil assets was pieced together by the World Bank. For each country the World Bank collected the data on discoveries, mineral by mineral. Angola, for example, had already discovered many millions of barrels of oil in its territory. The World Bank then multiplied the known reserves of each mineral by its world price and added them up into a valuation of each country's natural assets. Inevitably some countries were much more fortunate than others. Some, like Brunei and Kuwait had huge natural assets and very few people: the lucky citizens are natural millionaires. More generally, the snapshot shows that natural assets appear to be very unequally distributed around the world.

Luck clearly plays an important part. Tiny countries can find themselves either sitting atop of an oil well or completely empty-handed. But over a sufficiently large geographic area luck should tend to even out. Remember those four quadrants of the planet. By the time we have aggregated up to those vast quadrants it would be surprising if there were very large differences between them. Even if one natural asset tended to be clustered in a particular quadrant, we would expect that by the law of averages the other quadrants would be more fortunate with other natural assets. You would expect luck to even out, but it hasn't. While delving into that 2000 snapshot of natural assets, my colleague Anke Hoeffer and I stumbled across a simple but profoundly important revelation. Before revealing what it was I want to stay with the opening of the American West.

When the West was opened up, government was pretty thin on the ground. The American government therefore chose a highly distinctive approach to the discovery of hidden assets. It can best be described as the rule of "finders-keepers." The government licensed plots to prospectors who then owned what they found.

The finders-keepers rule may in important respects be an improvement upon lawlessness, but it gives rise to needless inequality and is also likely to be inefficient. The implications for inequality are pretty clear. My wife's great-great-uncle struck gold and his descendants are still living well off it; other gold diggers died in the attempt. The value of the natural assets, or at least the excess of their value over the cost of mining them, is captured by prospectors instead of being spread more widely.

The inefficiency is more subtle. It arises because the chances of striking lucky on a plot are increased if neighboring plots have had lucky strikes. The most profitable strategy is to acquire as many plots as possible and leave them idle until someone else makes a discovery. Owners of plots that stand idle are free-riding on the efforts of others. This produces the economics of a gold rush. Whole territories may be neglected for many years, and then prospected in a surge following the first discovery. Both the period of neglect and the surge are inefficient. The period of neglect arises from a standard public goods problem: knowledge is a public good and so the outcome is a stalemate in which no one risks the costs of acquiring knowledge. Eventually, a lucky strike occurs and in response people crowd into search, lowering the chances of discovery for each other. Recall that dire prediction of basic economics: people will spend time and money in search so long as the expected returns exceed the costs of searching. As they crowd in, reducing each individual chance of a discovery, most of this search is wasted activity. The total costs of the search approach the value of the resources to be extracted. The finders-keepers rule thus produces a long period during which private returns to search are below their social value, followed by a short period in which they exceed their social value.

To avoid the fate of the buffalo, or the inefficiency and inequality inherent in a gold rush, societies other than America have chosen to vest the initial ownership of natural assets collectively. The apex of collective action is government, and so governments decide the fate of natural assets. This makes them distinctive. The modern economics of production, as exemplified by a standard economics textbook, has little time for government. Output is generated by labor and capital, which is managed by firms. Government remains offstage because it is irrelevant to the analysis. In contrast, government is central to the effective management of natural assets.

Government is going to loom large, but what should it do? It has to manage natural assets because it cannot evade initial ownership. Although in this respect natural assets are distinctive, they are like other assets in two other respects: they can be depleted and their price is volatile. Managing the depletion and volatility of natural assets is not easy. The analogous decisions for financial assets support a huge industry from which New York and London derive much of their income. In contrast, although the management of natural assets pose at least as many complex problems, decisions lie not with an elite of experts (however much we may now doubt their credentials) but with governments, many of them the least competent governments on earth.

The social construction of rights over natural assets is inescapably a value-conferring activity and so it is liable to attract rent-seeking, or more colloquially, pork-barrel politics. This sort of politics can be so dysfunctional that a society ends up worse off than if it had not attempted to manage its natural assets in the first place. The key question is how to avoid such politics.

Of course, in a democracy, the government is answerable to voters. However, in order to vote you have to be a citizen, and indeed an adult. With respect to having a say as to the fate of the Brazilian rain forest Daniel is doubly disenfranchised: he is the wrong nationality and the wrong age. While I don't think that Daniel should be given the vote in Brazil, I do see his point of view. Is the Brazilian rain forest owned by the current generation of Brazilian voters?

Posing it in that way muddles up two distinct issues: Brazilians versus the rest of us, and the current generation of adults versus the future. Both matter. Should Brazilian voters have power of decision over the rain forest? Potentially, the power of decision should be situated either higher up or lower down. It should be higher up—not limited simply to Brazil—if we think that the rain forest is valuable to the entire world. This was clearly what Daniel has in mind in feeling that his own rights are being infringed. But there are also passionate advocates of placing the power of decision lower down: the rain forest belongs to its local inhabitants who have collectively sustained it, and who depend upon it. So, where should rights be lodged: locally, nationally or globally? For this we need an ethical framework. As an economist I have been reared to use the ethical framework of Utilitarianism.

The Greatest Happiness of the Greatest Number

The big idea in Utilitarianism is that the benchmark for ethical action is to achieve "the greatest happiness of the greatest number." Modern economics is an immensely sophisticated edifice which has thoroughly chewed over the difficulties of how societies might best set their goals. But when economics is applied to practical problems all this sophistication is set aside: we are trained simply to solve problems in which something has to be maximized. Utilitarianism lends itself to this approach: maximize the happiness of mankind. Applied to a problem such as how to assign the ownership of natural assets, Utilitarian economics simply adds up the happiness—or "utility"—of each individual. In order to sum these utilities it needs to make some assumptions. The big one is that each particular amount of income, say, $4,000 per month, generates the same amount of "utility" for each individual, and that every extra dollar generates less utility than the previous dollar.

This ethical framework is actually pretty radical: for a given overall size of the cake, the ideal distribution of the slices would be complete and universal equality. That would achieve the "greatest happiness of the greatest number," or "maximize the sum of utilities" as an economist would express it. This is because the last dollar spent by a rich person generates less utility than the last dollar generated by a poorer person. Peter Singer, the eminent Utilitarian philosopher, brilliantly sets out its implications for charity in his recent book, *The Life You Can Save*. How can you justify spending your money on yourself when you could spend it on others who would get so much more utility from it? Utilitarianism underlies redistributive taxation: income tax should be as high as possible subject only to its disincentive effect which makes the cake smaller. The ethical drivers are universalism and need, albeit tempered by practical constraints.

For choices in the exploitation of natural assets, such as the rain forest and oil, and natural liabilities such as carbon, the key distributional issues are inter-generational. The Utilitarian economist applies exactly the same ethical norms of universalism and need when deciding between the present generation and future generations. People as yet unborn count for the same as people alive today, however far in the future they might live. They don't have a vote, but to the

Utilitarian that is just a design flaw in democracy. Future people only count for less to the extent that they are going to be richer than we are in which case giving more money to them is not such a good idea. The actual balance between saving for the future and consuming nature now depends upon trading off the fact that money saved grows to be worth more in the future, against the fact that in the future extra consumption will generate less utility. The Utilitarian would say precisely the same about any temporary influx of money, whether it derived from the exploitation of natural assets or, for example, foreign aid.

To be fair to Utilitarian economists, there is one further reason why they would accept that those future people should count for less than us: they might not exist. A meteor might hit the Earth and do to us what one did to the dinosaurs. That beckoning extinction is factored into the calculations of Utilitarian economists working on climate change: if the future might not exist then this reduces the value of transferring happiness to future generations.

In some respects Utilitarianism as applied by economists is a noble vision. Basing decisions on universalism and need is certainly equitable. But it faces two overwhelming drawbacks. It is radically at variance with the ethics that prevail in most societies and so stands no chance of being their democratic choice. Further, it brooks no scope for variation. The same ethical code applies everywhere and always. If you are starting to get the feeling that economic Utilitarianism is best suited for Disneyland, I am inclined to agree. I have come to believe that it is an inappropriate framework for thinking about natural assets and liabilities.

The Ethics of Custody

There is an alternative. The environmental movement has recognized that ordinary people are willing to accept obligations concerning the natural world. This is not because they can be persuaded of the virtues of economic Utilitarianism. They are guided by ethical codes that are both richer and more varied than Utilitarianism allows for, and within those various ethical codes most people recognize nature as special. Their attitudes to nature can be common even if their overall ethics are diverse. The attempt to impose a common Utilitarian ethics across societies with radically different values is unlikely to be successful. Fortunately, it is also unnecessary.

In popular ethics the enemy of the Utilitarian principle of universalism is *propinquity*. This is a quaint way of saying that people who are closer to you matter to you more: family and friends matter more than people you have never met. This is a notion that most modern economists reject. Yet even the founding philosopher of Utilitarianism, Jeremy Bentham, accepted that propinquity was a legitimate sentiment. He recognized that propinquity applied between time periods as well as within a time period. As surveys confirm, we simply do not care for people who will live in the future as much as we care for ourselves. The more distant the future, the weaker are our sympathies with it.

It is easy to understand why we evolved with an instinct for propinquity. In all sorts of situations our chances for survival increase if we help our family and neighbors. Should we regard it as some psychological flaw in our make-up? Should we aspire to be angels, caring about everyone equally? Nicholas Stern, who has pioneered much of the economic analysis of climate change, accepts that sentiments of propinquity were evolved because they were functional. He also argues that this was because historically our needs were purely local. The new environmental challenges are global and so our evolved instincts are indeed inadequate for the global cooperation that is now necessary.

But understanding why sentiments of propinquity arose does not provide economists or governments with a license to override them. They are now hardwired into what it means to be a human being. Economic Utilitarianism is, in fact, much better suited to a population of ants than to a population of people. Ants are entirely willing to sacrifice themselves individually for the collective good. That is how they evolved. But it is really no good wishing that humans fit the economic model as well as ants. We simply have to accept the crooked timber of humanity for what it is.

One institution towers over the struggle between the competing claims of universalism and propinquity: the nation state. A nation provides people with a common identity, an imagined community, and within it to varying degrees the state implements universalism. Beyond the frontiers of the nation propinquity dominates. The most dramatic demonstration of how abrupt the transition between rival ethical values can be is Europe. Famously, European nations accept by far the highest levels of internal redistributive taxation found in the world: around 40 percent of income is taxed. Further, for the past fifty years most of its nations have been bound together in a Union which has the power to tax and redistribute. Yet, although income levels vary considerably between the nations within the Community, redistribution of income between member states is negligible. The pan-European tax rate is merely 1 percent of income, and virtually all of this is redistributed within the country which has originally paid the taxes. Indeed, this became an ethical sticking point for British membership of the Community: beyond a low threshold, the taxes that Britain pays to the Community can be used only for payments back to Britain. Hence, even the passage from the nation to the pooled sovereignty among the democracies of the European Union takes us beyond the domain in which the Utilitarian principle of universalism is regarded as acceptable. Propinquity abounds in the European Community.

In popular ethics the enemy of the Utilitarian principle of need, however, is not propinquity but the right of *possession*. In 2009 the Rowntree Foundation, a Quaker charity with a long record of insightful social inquiry, surveyed British attitudes to inequality. It was astonished by what it found. In essence, ordinary people did not perceive that inequality was necessarily unfair. Those poor people who had been unlucky were indeed deserving of help from those who had been lucky. But those who had been feckless were not deserving of help from those who had been prudent. People who had worked hard and been prudent were entitled to enjoy what they earned. Economic Utilitarianism is willing to go along with this as a practical necessity. Were people not allowed to keep the fruits of their work, they would not go to the trouble of earning it. However, according to popular ethics it is more than that: effort confers rights of possession.

If natural assets have no natural owners, our rights of possession over them are much weaker than our rights over man-made assets. Man-made assets are the product of our creativity, and this confers powerful rights of ownership. What I have created I am free to give and to sell. Initial acts of creation are the basis of most property rights. Even within nations the Utilitarian principle of universalism can co-exist with the right of possession conferred by creativity, though the balance might vary. Almost all nations have redistributive taxation but individual tax rates are tempered not just by practical but by ethical considerations. But natural assets are not the result of creativity. In the absence of rights of possession stemming from creativity, who should benefit from natural assets? The Utilitarian principles of universalism and need suggest that everyone should do so. Those principles face only the counter-principle of propinquity: whoever is closest to the natural asset should benefit.

But the tug of propinquity is not like the tug of gravity, diminishing steadily mile-by-mile according to distance. The shared identity of a nation and the organizational capabilities of the state create a towering cliff. Usually they are sufficiently strong to overcome differential propinquity within its boundaries: the state enforces a universal ownership of natural assets. Only at the border does propinquity prevail: people from other nations have no claim on those natural assets.

Here, the sentiment of propinquity is compounded by the absence of an institution equivalent to the state which could enforce the redistribution of natural assets between nations. This limitation on universalism increases inequality. For example, because Africa is split up into so many nations, and the ownership rights over natural assets are accorded to nations, their per capita distribution is inevitably highly unequal. Citizens of Equatorial Guinea have radically more natural assets than citizens of Ethiopia despite the fact that both are African. Nonetheless we should be thankful that nations are there to counter yet narrower claims of propinquity. Were subnational groups to acquire ownership by virtue of their proximity to natural assets distribution will be even more unequal. For example, the tiny island nation of São Tomé and Príncipe, located in the Gulf of Guinea off the western equatorial coast of Africa, has recently discovered oil, which benefits the 100,000 Africans who are its citizens. However, the oil is closer to Príncipe than to São Tomé, and, predictably, its 8,000 inhabitants have claimed the ownership.

If you think that the inhabitants of Príncipe are a little selfish, it gets worse: as valuable natural assets are discovered borders start to change. The tug-of-war between propinquity and universalism is currently being played out in the Arctic. Geologists now suspect that there may be 90 billion barrels of oil beneath the icecap: who should own it? One sure sign of greedy opportunism is when the discovery of valuable natural resources leads to a demand to change borders. The Arctic is currently international territory, but following the discovery the nations bordering on the Arctic have started to assert their claims.

Where propinquity rules claims need not stop at the national level: greed drives a localization of identity. Sure enough, Greenland, which is a territory of Denmark, is now asserting a greater degree of independence. The claims of propinquity go further still: the Inuit, whose homeland stretches from the northeastern tip of Russia and across Alaska, northern Canada, and into Greenland, claim rights to the oil beneath their kayaks.

Until the discovery of oil off the coast of Scotland in the mid-1960s the Scottish Nationalist Party had only negligible support for its goal of secession from the rest of Britain. When the oil price leapt in 1973 the vote for the party promptly soared: by the following year it was commanding 30 percent of the Scottish vote. But as the oil price came back down, support faded: by the late 1990s with the price down to $10 a barrel the SNP appeared a spent force. It was saved by the global commodity boom: in 2007, with the oil price heading toward $100, the SNP achieved its big breakthrough, becoming the largest party in Scotland. The Welsh National Party tried to do the same thing with rainwater, but as any tourist knows, Britain is not short of rain.

While I believe that national rights should be respected, there is a sharp distinction to be made between the borders of nations defined by history and those defined by greedy grasping of natural assets. The natural assets that lie beyond a nation's historic borders should not belong to its citizens any more than paddling a canoe above an oilfield should confer rights over the oil beneath. Although most of the planet's natural assets are located within national borders, those that are in international territory should remain international: they belong to all of us.

Propinquity and practicality ally to warrant nations appropriating the natural assets within their borders, but there is no equivalent ethical maneuver that will permit the present to appropriate them from the future. Natural assets have a unique physical location: if they are in my country they are not in yours. But by virtue of being assets they do not have a unique temporal location. As we wave gleefully across the national boundary we can shout to our neighbors without a sense of guilt, "these are ours, not yours." But we cannot, without guilt, leave a message to the future, saying in effect "they were ours, not yours." There is no inter-temporal equivalent to the national border that distinguishes one society from another. Individually there is admittedly an (unfortunate) inter-temporal boundary between life and death, but that is individual: we are not all going to die at once. Natural assets are owned collectively by the society, and the society rolls on and on.

We have arrived at an ethics of nature in which plunder can take two distinct forms. In one, natural assets that should belong to all the citizens of a nation are expropriated by the few for their private benefit. In the other, natural assets that should belong to all generations are expropriated by those citizens currently alive for their own benefit.

Individual people, and indeed whole societies, can differ radically on wider ethical issues: the importance of propinquity versus universalism; need versus the rights of possession. These differences essentially concern how societies allocate their created assets. But they can all recognize these two forms of plunder as unethical. Usually, national identity is sufficiently strong for the natural assets within the nation to be held in common. What is held in common is not a right of ownership but a right of custody, however. We have no more right to enjoy these assets than the future generations of the nation. If we use up a natural asset we must provide those future generations with compensation.

The Middle East has a culture and ethical values quite different from the Western tradition, yet it recognizes that natural assets should be held in custody. Three decades ago Kuwait had the natural asset of oil and pretty much nothing else. That generation of Kuwaitis took the view that they were not at liberty to use oil revenues only for consumption. Instead, they created a financial fund for future generations. Future Kuwaitis will no longer have oil, but they will have other assets. In the radically different culture of Zambia the depleted copper is not matched by any assets accumulated for future generations. But this does not reflect a difference in the ethics of nature: as a Zambian friend expressed it, "When the copper has run out, what will our children say about us?"

To sum up, we do not have an obligation to preserve every natural asset, but nor are we at liberty to plunder natural wealth without regard for the future. We have an ethical responsibility to bequeath to unborn generations either the natural assets bequeathed to us, or other assets of equivalent value. Our ethical responsibilities for natural assets are thus fundamentally economic: nature is a valuable asset. Natural assets are special, but not so special that they cannot be used. We are free to use them. If we do so without leaving equivalent value, however, we are guilty of plunder. The obligation of custody is not grounded in some complicated Utilitarian calculation of how utility might be maximized. It is grounded in our recognition of the rights of others.

Custody is not as restrictive as preservation. The romantic wing of environmentalism sees nature as so special that we are merely its curators, and here I part company. Biodiversity is a good thing, but within the context of our survival, not as an end in itself. We are not here to serve nature; nature is here to serve us. In case this sounds excessively materialist, I think that Christian thinking comes to much the same conclusion through the concept of stewardship. Mankind has "dominion" over the natural world: it is there for us to make something of it, not merely to preserve it in aspic. One of the parables of Jesus, told in Luke, is of the nobleman who goes away, leaving money with each of his servants. One merely preserves the money, literally wrapping it up in a napkin. Upon the nobleman's return he is chastised. The ones who are praised are those who put the money to good use. We can do the same with nature. Most especially we can use nature to transform the plight of the bottom billion.

I share with environmentalists a less pessimistic view of human nature than is routine among economists. Economic models typically characterize people as selfish and greedy. Polarized between an ethical framework in which people ought to behave like saints, and a view of human nature in which they actually behave more like psychopaths, economists are often unenthusiastic about democracy. They prefer an authoritarian government that tells people what to do, and takes its advice from economists. Whereas economists rely upon technical briefings with the right government officials, environmentalists have periodically mobilized ordinary citizens into mass action before which governments and companies have quaked. It is not necessary for ordinary people to adopt the ethics of saintly ants in order for them to want their governments to be custodians of nature rather than plunderers.

Should Brazilian Voters Rule the Rain Forest?

What does this imply about the present generation of Brazilian voters? In a true democracy the government must be accountable to the electorate and each eligible citizen has one vote. Future generations do not and indeed cannot have votes. But Brazilian voters should recognize their ethical obligations to future Brazilians. They are not at liberty to cut the rain forest without leaving an equivalent asset for future generations. If they neglect this responsibility they can indeed legitimately be pilloried for plundering the natural world.

This is not the end of the ethical responsibilities of Brazilian voters. I have been dismissive of Inuit claims over the oil beneath the icecap, but I am not dismissive of the interests of the inhabitants of the rain forest. The rain forest is their habitat, and has only come down to us because they have not plundered it. If it is felled, their entire culture will disappear. Felling it might benefit other Brazilians, but it is liable to be quite dramatically at their expense. While they should not have the rights to oil beneath the forest, as a community they surely have rights of ownership to the forest which is their home. I do not mean that the communities of the rain forest should necessarily be preserved in perpetuity. This would be to condemn these peoples never to integrate with the rest of mankind—to treat them as anthropological curiosities. But the confrontation between the dwellers of the rain forest and modernity is acutely difficult, to be handled gradually and carefully: the history of such encounters abounds in tragedy. I suspect that over time the forest dwellers will vote with their feet to be part of Brazilian society, just as the last Aborigines have now chosen to leave the isolation of the Australian bush. But forced expulsion through the elimination of their habitat is ethically wrong. Although many of the beneficiaries of the felling of the rain forest have been poor Brazilians in need of land, hence justified on the Utilitarian calculus of need, the redistribution from forest dwellers infringes their rights of possession.

Brazilian voters have one further ethical responsibility, as the forest is felled and burned carbon is emitted. While the revenues from the felled wood and cleared land accrue now to Brazil, future generations inherit this liability. So, even if the current generation of Brazilians leaves adequate replacement assets for future Brazilian citizens, they are guilty of plundering the citizens of the rest of the world to benefit their own nationals. Environmentalists around the world are right to be concerned, and Daniel had good reason to be angry.

Nature as Asset

Nature as Asset

CHAPTER 3

Cursed by Nature? The Politics of Natural Assets

ARE NATURAL ASSETS A CURSE? In *The Bottom Billion* I argued why I thought they often did more harm than good to the poorest countries. But the real measure is not just the damage they cause, but their harm relative to their potential. Natural resources are the largest assets available to these societies. Their known natural capital has been estimated to be worth double their produced capital. The failure to harness natural capital is the single-most important missed opportunity in economic development. Since writing *The Bottom Billion* I have accumulated more research on the subject, as have many others. Indeed, whether an abundance of natural assets is a blessing or a curse is currently one of the disputes raging among economists.

There are some high-visibility instances of natural assets appearing to ruin a country: Sierra Leone's diamonds, for example, seemed to shred the fabric of that society to pieces; Nigeria's oil fueled the corruption of the political class. But are these just outliers? After all, Botswana harnessed its diamonds to produce the fastest growing economy in the world, and Norway used its oil to achieve the world's highest living standard. The question becomes whether there really is a "resource curse," and whether, if it does exist, it is limited to countries with deeper problems.

I have come to regard this as the most crucial issue in the struggle to transform the poorest societies. The revenues that they could get from natural assets are enormous, dwarfing any conceivable flows of aid. They could certainly be transformative. If they deliver, any efforts to inhibit the extraction of natural assets from the poorest countries are not simply counterproductive but irresponsible, impeding the path out of poverty. If, on the other hand, natural assets backfire, then there is an argument for leaving them in the ground. There would indeed be the basis for an alliance between the environmental lobby, pressing for natural assets to be conserved, and the development lobby, fighting to end mass poverty.

The existence of the resource curse is disputed. Indeed, as I sat down to write this chapter, a journalist from *New York Times* phoned; he was doing a story on the subject. He had just talked to Robert Conrad at Duke, who has recently shown that on average resource-rich countries have higher incomes than those that are resource-scarce. Like Bob, I have been investigating statistically whether a resource curse exists. Although Bob is right about the average income of resource-rich countries, this is by no means the end of the story.

I teamed up with the young Dutch economist Benedikt Goderis who quit his potentially lucrative niche as a researcher in financial economics at Cambridge to join me in Oxford working on the poorest countries. Since he has made possible what you are about to read you can judge the loss to society. We based our analysis on forty years of economic performance for each commodity-exporting country in the world. The work took three years. Just as we thought we had finished we discovered we had made a mistake that sent us back to the computer to re-analyze everything. (I remember Benedikt saying, "I'm just off to kill myself." Fortunately, he went off to the pub instead.) Producing new results stretched us to the limits of our patience and our competence. Neither Bob Conrad's work nor our own are the first statistical analyses of the curse question. One previous study compared the growth rates of countries with and without natural resources. It found that resource-rich countries grew more slowly than resource-poor countries, which was apparent evidence for the resource curse. However, this type of approach, known as "cross-section analysis," has severe limitations and is treated with considerable skepticism by most economists. In essence, it cannot interpret what is causing what. After all, if there is a resource curse it must happen over time: the discovery of natural assets should in some important respect worsen the economy. Hence, what is needed is not a comparison between countries but a comparison of the same country before and after an increase in its revenues from natural resources.

One common critique of the resource-curse hypothesis argues that the association between resource-dependence and slow growth can arise even without it. Suppose that we start from a random assignment of natural-resource endowments. Some countries get a lot and others a little. Now suppose that for reasons entirely unrelated to this initial resource endowment some countries grow faster than others. After a few decades we will find that the countries that are now most dependent upon natural resources will tend to be the ones that have grown slowly. This is simply because the fast growers will have grown out of resource-dependence: nonresource income will be high. Superficially, it will look like the resource curse, but this would be a misinterpretation. Economists refer to this problem as "endogeneity." (They could equally have called it "the horse and cart problem" but it would not have sounded so impressive. In the familiar game of thinking up clever collective names, nobody has ever suggested "a modesty of economists.")

In this particular case the solution is straightforward: instead of measuring resource-dependence as resource revenues relative to income you measure it by resources per person. Sometimes this indeed makes a difference. America, for example, has a lot of resources per person, but because the rest of its economy has grown so successfully it does not have a particularly high share of resource revenues in income.

Benedickt and I ended up using the relatively new statistical technique of "co-integration," which had not previously been deployed on this question. This approach enabled us to tease out both the short-term effect of commodity prices on growth, and the longer-term effects on the level of income. Using it, we were able to reconcile an apparent contradiction between previous crosssection and time-series studies: both were correct, but within different time-frames. Our preliminary results were sufficiently disturbing that I was promptly invited by the U.S. Treasury to present them at the G20 meeting of finance ministers that it was hosting.

Commodity Booms: Hunky Dory or Humpty Dumpty?

In the short term the extraction of natural assets is hunky dory. It significantly raises growth rates. For example, during a boom, a doubling in the world price of a single exported commodity can increase output in a country's entire economy over the next three years by around 5 percent. The economy's output goes up across the board. In one sense this increase in output is the icing on the cake of a commodity boom. Even if output were unaffected incomes would go up because the same amount of exports will now buy more imports. Oil that in 1998 fetched only $10 a barrel was fetching over $140 a decade later, so oil exporters could import more despite the fact that output had remained unchanged. This is what Bob Conrad was finding: the exploitation of natural assets usually raised income even if it did not increase output. But in a developing economy that extra output is not the icing, it is the cake itself. Without extra output the bonanza is unsustainable. Still, at least in the short term, an increase in the world price of a commodity confers on exporters a double bonanza: both income and output go up.

So much for the short run, what about the long run? John Maynard Keynes, the man who invented "Keynesian" economics, dismissed the long run with the quip, "in the long run we're all dead." This aptly describes what we find lies in store for commodity exporters. We investigated the long-run effect of commodity booms for three different types of commodities: oil, other nonagricultural products, and agricultural products. Obviously, the effect depends upon how important the commodity is to the country's economy. Let's start with oil, the most important of all the commodities. For a country like Nigeria, whose oil exports are around a third of its economy, if the oil price doubles after a quarter of a century the level of economic output sinks to only around two-thirds of what it would otherwise have been. Oil is more important to Angola's economy—constituting around two thirds of total output. The adverse effect is correspondingly more severe: if the oil price doubles the long-run level of total economic output halves relative to what it would otherwise have been.

These effects on output carry a disturbing message. But are they unique to oil? Perhaps oil booms produce particularly awful results either because of the behavior of the international oil companies, or because local politicians get delusions of grandeur and squander the proceeds on luxury and white elephant projects. We find that the adverse consequences of oil, however, are not significantly different from those of the other nonagricultural commodities. Copper, bauxite, coltan: the exporters of these commodities share the long-term fate of the oil exporters—a massive loss of output. These results suggest the existence of a resource curse in output, which in turn implies a huge loss of potential income. After all, the extraction of natural assets should enable output to expand, not force it to contract.

The question is how far the resource curse generalizes from oil to other nonagricultural commodities such as copper. And does it apply quite generally to primary agricultural commodities, whose prices can be as volatile as those for oil and copper. We found a radical difference between agricultural and nonagricultural commodities: the long-run effect of higher agricultural commodity prices is positive. That result provides a clue to understanding the resource curse.

But first, let me take you further on my own core concern, which is Africa. At present commodity exports represent 30 percent of Africa's GDP, so are hugely important. I wanted to see whether Africa's relationship between commodity prices and the growth of commodity-exporting countries was unique. The issue matters: Africa is distinctive in being more dependent upon commodity exports than other regions, aside from the Middle East. The question is whether African management of natural assets has been different in whether they are harnessed for the growth of output.

In fact, Africa's management did not prove to be significantly different. This did not surprise me. I have looked at several dimensions in which Africa appears to be unique and generally find that its nations, when faced with the same challenges and opportunities, behave pretty much like most other nations. Africa's outcomes have been distinctive because the structure of its economies and societies is distinctive: it is the problems facing Africans, rather than the choices they have made about those problems, that have been distinctive.

We needed to learn whether Africa was different because we wanted to know whether we could predict the consequences of the recent commodity booms for Africa by using results from the rest of the world. That it is not significantly different enabled us to simulate those consequences. We took the fourteen major African commodity-exporting countries. Between 1996 and 2006 the price of oil more than tripled and the price of other nonagricultural commodity exports of these countries on average more than doubled. The consequences of these increases are both important in themselves and for grasping the general implications of our analysis.

We find that in the short term commodity booms added considerably to the growth rate of Africa's commodity exporters. By 2009, we estimated, output in these countries would be around 10 percent higher than had prices remained at their levels of the late 1990s. Of course, incomes have risen by much more than this because each barrel of oil, or whatever, was exchanging for more imports: an effect known as a gain in the terms of trade. For a country that was initially exporting 30 percent of GDP, a doubling of export prices directly added 30 percent to the purchasing power of income, so that the combined quantity and terms of trade effects amount to around a 40-percent gain relative to what would have been the case had export prices not changed. It was indeed evident that the short-term effects were decidedly hunky dory.

But our forecast for the long-term effects was entirely different. If Africa were to follow the global historical pattern, the adverse effects of the commodity boom would set in only slowly, but by 2024 output would be *down* by a quarter relative to what it would have been. This is a grim result. A major commodity boom has the potential to be transforming. It is an income-injection beyond the dreams of aid agencies. Properly used it can lift growth and income to levels at which the risk of violence and social unrest becomes negligible.

The present commodity boom could bring peace to many previously unstable countries. You might think that the worst that could happen would be for the revenues to be entirely frittered away. Yet we find worse: in the long term the economy severely contracts. This is not quite the same as saying that the society would have been better off without the revenues. As before, the dramatic decline in long-term output is only part of the overall effect on income: as long as prices remain high there is still the gain due to the terms of trade. The economy is producing much less than it would have done without the high export prices, but what it does produce is worth more. The net effect is that income is more or less where it would have been without the commodity bonanza. The resource curse, in other words, is predominantly a missed opportunity.

This, then, is the prognosis. If history repeats itself the recent commodity booms will in the long term, at best, create missed opportunities; at worst, they might fundamentally derail societies. It is thus of first-order importance that history not be repeated. The first step in avoiding a repetition is to understand the mechanisms by which past opportunities turned to dust. For this we need to move on from prognosis to diagnosis.

Diagnosis

There is no shortage of contending explanations for the resource curse. Benedikt and I trawled through the pertinent economic and political science literature and arranged them into six groups. Most of the explanations sounded plausible enough and each was supported by evidence. From what we read, however, there seemed to be no way of telling which ones were most persuasive: each researcher had mounted his own plausible hobby horse and off he rode. We therefore decided to be systematic. We would not only generate a prognosis but discriminate among competing diagnoses.

One key way of distinguishing between them involved the different effects agricultural and nonagricultural commodity price booms had. Both types of commodities have booms, but the long-term consequences of the agricultural booms are benign. The resource curse is entirely confined to the nonagricultural commodities. Agricultural commodities are intrinsically renewable, whereas nonagricultural commodities intrinsically depletable. Why does this matter? Because almost all renewable output has already been renewed and so is the harvest from previous investment. Coffee exports come from past investments in coffee trees. Competition ensures that the returns on that investment are not significantly higher than for other activities. Coffee can be grown in many places so that location cannot command much of a premium. The revenues from agricultural commodities are therefore predominantly a return on past investment and current work. In contrast, minerals are valuable over-and-above the investment and work needed to extract them. Agricultural commodities, in short, are less subject to plunder than are minerals.

I do not want to paint an overly rosy picture of how naturally renewable commodities are managed. Sometimes they are indeed plundered. But the circumstances in which they are plundered are highly specific. For the present I am going to focus on those natural resources which can only be used once, and on why these depleting natural assets are so subject to plunder. The plunder of naturally renewable commodities will be the subject of part III.

The value of depleting natural assets over-and-above their cost of extraction belongs to citizens; governments should capture it on their behalf. Typically governments are keen to capture at least some of the value, whether or not they then use it to benefit ordinary citizens. The only society in the world which has decided to leave the value almost entirely with whoever might be lucky enough to find them is the United States, which adopted the "finders keepers" approach to prospecting. Everywhere else at least part of the value from the extraction of natural assets accrues to governments (whereas the revenues from agricultural commodities largely accrue to farmers as the return on their investment and work). This suggests that the resource curse might be connected to something that is specific to the public management of revenues, to governance.

Governance is a slippery concept. In the end, to measure it, we relied upon a commercial rating called the International Country Risk Guide (ICRG), which is calculated annually and made available to international companies for a price. Our hope was that since the ICRG had survived for many years as a business, its ratings might have been based on substantive content. Either that or it has been thriving on collective delusion. (Given the recent collective performance of the other major risk-rating agencies, the latter possibility cannot be excluded.) However, were the company basically selling random numbers packaged as information, the data would have had no significant effect. Adding random numbers to a statistical analysis is just adding "noise": the statistics will tell you that you have been wasting your time. In fact, when we added the ICRG governance series the results told us that we had struck gold. Essentially, if a country has decent governance, far from there being a resource curse, the long-run effects of high commodity prices reinforce the short-run effects. The resource curse is confined to countries with weak governance.

At this point we started to worry about the horse and cart problem again. Perhaps it was just that governance deteriorated in response to the discovery of resource rents rather than starting that way. We tackled this in two ways, one simple the other fancy. The simple way was to measure governance only by the first year for which the ICRG measure was available. This was 1985. Any deterioration in governance due to resource rents after that date was excluded from the analysis. Our results didn't change: weak governance was a killer, whereas with decent governance resource rents had beneficial long-term effects. Based on this diagnosis, it is initial variations in governance that account for why oil has enhanced the Norwegian economy while wrecking the Nigerian.

How weak is "weak," and how decent is "decent"? The dividing line occurred where Portugal had been in 1985. At the time, only eleven years out of dictatorship and revolution, Portugal was still one of the worst governed countries in Europe but was nevertheless a functioning democracy. Botswana was a little above the boundary. Governance in Botswana has been honest, although below OECD standards. For example, although the country's government has many democratic features, there has never been an alternation of power. However, Botswana has indeed been better governed than other low-income commodity exporters. Having resolved the horse and cart problem we then subjected the results to a range of tests designed to detect spurious results. The tests left the results intact: as far as we can tell, initially weak governance is the key cause of the resource curse.

But "governance" still remains a very imprecise concept. How does poor governance dissipate the opportunities provided by resource revenues? Again, within limits, our statistical approach enabled us to tease out some answers. The method involved adding plausible explanations until we found some that were themselves significant and which collectively eliminated the significance of governance.

When economists consider the resource curse they think of "Dutch Disease," so called because the Dutch economy was the first recognized instance. The discovery of North Sea gas squeezed existing exports while the Dutch currency appreciated. A boom in commodity exports tends to appreciate the exchange rate and this in turn dampens growth. At least qualitatively, Dutch Disease therefore looked a likely explanation so we decided to test for it by adding a measure of the exchange rate to our analysis. It indeed had a substantial effect but again was conditional upon governance: in a well-governed country natural-resource revenues did not lead to massive appreciation of the exchange rate, whereas in a badly governed country they did.

Despite the fuss that economists have made over it for the past thirty years, Dutch Disease is not inevitable. For example, revenues can be spent on infrastructure that makes other exports more competitive. Malaysia used its earnings from resource exports to diversify its economy and now has a wide range of nonresource exports. It attracts more foreign investment per capita than any other developing country. Botswana used its diamonds to become the fastest growing economy in the world. Norway used its oil to become Europe's richest economy.

In addition to the exchange rate, key mechanisms of the resource curse work through excessive public and private consumption, and insufficient investment. Although consumption and investment largely "account" for the governance effect in the statistical sense, they do not account for all of it. It is difficult to build good empirical proxies that are available for many countries over many years, and so our statistical approach is inevitably highly constrained. Most probably, the measurable routes stand in for other processes

CURSED BY NATURE? **49**

that we cannot properly measure. Indeed, in terms of data our approach was demanding: to include something as an explanation we needed a measure that was comparable across most countries in the world over many years. That is why, for example, we were not able to incorporate redistributions to favored groups, although this is a pretty plausible explanation for what happens when resource revenues meet weak governance.

Politics: Testing the Neo-con Agenda

Given that we know that poor governance is the key to the resource curse, does history have to repeat itself? Preventing that is the only reason why our research would matter.

It is time to bring the politics back into the analysis. The work I have just described was based on data for the period 1963–2003 and for most of this period politics in the bottom billion meant dictatorship. The wasted booms of the 1970s were usually overseen by autocrats. The spread of democracy following the fall of the Soviet Union in 1991 changed all that. The past, therefore, may not be a good guide to how the resource booms of the new millennium will be managed. The spread of democracy may have improved governance sufficiently that the resource curse would be a thing of the past. This seemed the single most important question facing the societies of the bottom billion in the current decade.

I had started considering this question when I wrote *The Bottom Billion* and gave a brief account of the early results there. The work has now advanced to the point that I feel more confident about it. My colleague in this as in much of my research was Anke Hoeffer. We entitled our paper "Testing the Neo-con Agenda." This was not done tongue in cheek. A reasonable interpretation of the neoconservative justification for the invasion of Iraq is that it would bring democracy to the resource-rich Middle East. As we now know, the rationale for this objective received far less scrutiny than the military means used to achieve it. The question I wanted to investigate was whether, if a country is resource-rich, democracy is indeed exactly what the doctor ordered, at least on the criterion of economic performance.

Democracy generates accountability. Giving citizens votes should empower them to discipline governments into doing their best for the typical voter. I investigated this larger question of whether elections force governments to improve economic policy with Lisa Chauvet, a young French economist. Encouragingly, we found that elections worked: when governments were required to face the electorate they improved their economic policies. There is an important caveat, but superficially that result suggested that democratization might raise standards of governance in the resource-rich countries out of the range of the resource curse.

Yet I still wondered whether the discipline of elections could prove ineffective in resource-rich societies. One reason that it might is that resource revenues are special. Remember, natural assets have no natural owners, and thus ordinary citizens and businesses may not see themselves as owning them. Resource revenues are not perceived as income in the same way as the income earned from working is. Indeed, all too often, they are not seen at all; they accrue unnoticed to the government. When the state tries to tax away the earned income of workers or businesses it provokes opposition: people want to know how their money is being used. But the money that flows to the state from natural assets most probably does not arouse such opposition. Indeed, in many of the societies of the bottom billion the state has simply never been seen as providing ordinary citizens with public goods. From its colonial origins the state has been alien, and often a power to fear. In one local language

I have come across the very words used for "government" translate literally as "white man's job." The state's retention of resource revenues therefore does not provoke demands for scrutiny.

Part of the power of economics stems from its using the assumption of "maximizing behavior" to predict the consequences of some change in the world: the economist simply works out how the change would affect the "maximizing strategy." We are going to do that now with the question of how natural-resource revenues change the behavior of political leaders. Suppose—dread the thought—that our political leader is not a saint. Far from it. To put it crudely, he wants to embezzle as much as he can from the state. However, if the only source of public revenue is taxation, he faces a dilemma. He finds that as he forces tax rates up, people get increasingly angry that they are getting nothing in return: taxation provokes scrutiny and demands for honest government. So, the politician would prefer not to tax. But of course without taxation the public coffers are empty and so there is nothing to embezzle. The politician has to trade off the gains to government's coffers from higher taxes against the scrutiny that they provoke: he chooses the level of taxation at which embezzlement is maximized.

Imagine how the leader's decision problem changes if he has revenues from natural resources such as oil. Without resource revenues he set taxation such that he just broke even from the last little slice of tax. The additional scrutiny that he provoked exactly matched what he gained from the additional revenue. Now things are different. The resource revenue gives him a base of income that has not provoked much scrutiny. Taxing people's earned incomes as well will provoke scrutiny and this will eat into not only his capacity to embezzle this extra tax revenue but crucially, his capacity to embezzle the natural-resource revenue. Whatever scrutiny there is applies to expenditure and therefore covers all types of revenue.

The corrupt leader therefore has a much stronger incentive to keep taxes low. Indeed, he might decide not to tax at all; that way he can embezzle the highest possible proportion of the resource revenues.

In the model that we set up, what emerged was that the corrupt politician used the resource revenues dollar-for-dollar to reduce the taxation of earned income. That result is not inevitable; a more complicated model could have taxation falling by more or by less than the resource revenues. But the case of the simple model has a powerful corollary. If total revenue is no higher as a result of the resource rents, think what happens to the amount of public money that is spent to improve the lives of ordinary citizens. Since total revenue is unaltered, the additional money embezzled by the corrupt politician, thanks to the reduction in scrutiny, comes, dollar for dollar, at the expense of public spending. So, we would expect all the good things that well-used public money can buy, such as education and health care would actually diminish as a result of resource revenues. We might think of this both as a parable of what happens to a society over time after natural resources have been discovered, and as a prophecy of how a resource-rich country will differ from a resource-scarce country. Although I have told it as a story about money, we could equally well think of it as a story about "effort." The politician not only uses the lack of scrutiny to embezzle money, he uses it to avoid the difficult work of economic policy reform.

So much for economic analysis. At best it offers parables. But it also provides a counterpoint to the notion that giving people the vote will necessarily empower them to discipline their government. Our prediction was that democracy would work less well in resource-rich countries than in resource-scarce countries.

My work with Benedikt on the resource curse focused on the consequences of commodity revenues on the sustained growth of a country's economic output. Although there are various possible measures of performance by which we might want to judge a political system, growth still seemed the key issue. Growth is what the bottom billion have lacked, and it was what natural-resource revenues should be able to deliver. The question that Anke and I determined to address was how democracy affected the economic activity of resource-rich countries. We decided to average the annual growth of output over four-year periods, thereby ironing out short-term fluctuations. Our approach was to include as many countries as possible, for as long a time span as possible, investigating how resources and democracy affected growth. In particular, we wanted to know what happened when the two were combined, as in the resource-rich democracies. This sounds easier than it was. Our initial results were discouraging. In the absence of resources, democracy significantly increased growth; in the presence of resource wealth it significantly reduced growth. So resource revenues appeared to corrupt democratic politics, turning it from being an improvement on autocracy to being even worse. This was certainly consistent with the rather depressing analysis of how resource revenue might undermine accountability.

This was far from definitive. Still, there are many possible pitfalls in empirical research of this type and the issue that nowadays most exercises economists is the interpretation of causality. Potentially, democracy can be determined by economic performance rather than the other way around; or something else might be determining both whether a society was democratic and whether it grew. And our measure of whether a country was resource-rich posed serious problems. It was simply the value of natural-resource exports as a proportion of national income. This might sound fine, but a country which fails to grow because of poor governance will have a low income and so tend to have a high share of natural-resource exports.

This in turn would tend to give rise to a "result" that a high share of natural-resource exports "caused" slow growth. But it would be spurious.

In 2000 the World Bank made an inventory of known subsoil assets around the world. The known natural assets per country depend upon the discovery process. A country that has poor governance will tend not to engage in prospecting for resources and therefore have a low endowment of known natural assets per person. So known natural assets per person will tend to be lower in countries with poor governance. We thus have two potential measures of the natural-resource endowment of a country, each affected by governance but in opposite ways. Poor governance will tend to increase natural resources as a proportion of national income, but reduce natural resources per person. This is helpful because if our result survives using each measure then it is unlikely to be a spurious misreading of causality stemming from governance.

Allowing for the various causal possibilities involving democracy is much more difficult. We followed what other researchers had done: trying to use various independent characteristics which influenced whether a country was democratic but which were not related to whether or not it had natural assets. For example, we used a measure of the historic mortality rate of settlers. The rate strongly influenced how many settlers a country attracted, and in turn this influenced whether it became democratic. We pressed on with such robustness tests and kept coming up with the same result: democracy and natural-resource revenues were not good bedfellows. Fortunately the story then became less depressing. When we think of democracy we immediately think of elections. After all, they are the newsworthy event, the moment when ordinary citizens have power over the fate of their government. But in truth, those of us fortunate enough to have lived all our lives in a mature democracy only think of elections because we take so much else for granted. Democracy is not just elections; it is a whole set of rules that limit what government can do. In a mature democracy a government cannot loot the public purse because the entire budget process is highly transparent. In places where government is corrupt, the opposite is true. In Liberia prior to the present government of President Ellen Johnson-Sirleaf, ministers simply instructed the central bank to transfer money into their personal bank accounts. They took it for granted that there were no systems of scrutiny that could hold these blatantly crooked payments to account. Officials in the central bank, faced with such requests, knew that they had no choice but to comply. There was no mechanism to block these transfers, and if they tried they were taking their lives in their hands.

In a mature democracy the government cannot victimize its opponents, (however much it would like to do so), nor deny them a voice in the media. It cannot discriminate against them in jobs and public services. It cannot jail them. Any attempts to do so tend to backfire. Moreover, in a mature democracy the conduct of an election is clean, or at least irregularities are seldom sufficient to frustrate the intentions of voters. Again, when breaches occur there is sufficient popular outrage that the problem gets addressed. In sum, these restraints upon government are fundamental to democracy.

Political scientists try to measure these checks and balances. One such measure is the number of independent veto points that can block an instruction from a senior member of government, such as those payments by the Liberian central bank. Anke and I introduced this measure into our analysis and found that it had a dramatic effect. In resource-rich societies these checks and balances were distinctively beneficial. If a society had enough of them then democracy worked fine. In countries without significant resource wealth checks and balances did not seem to affect economic performance; elections worked well enough. The damage done to democracy in resource-rich countries stemmed from electoral competition. Whereas in societies without natural assets elections appeared to discipline governments into good economic performance, in countries with them the ensuing revenues appeared to undermine elections, unless offset by strong checks and balances.

So, resource-rich countries need particularly strong checks and balances. Unfortunately, they get precisely the opposite. We find that gradually, over the course of several decades, revenues from natural resources tend to erode checks and balances. It is not difficult to understand why: the checks and balances stand between politicians and plunder.

Elections are a potentially vital check on the abuse of power. What goes wrong with them in resource-rich countries? Trying to answer this has been my latest research, again with Anke. We built a global data set of more than seven hundred elections that distinguished between those that were reasonably well conducted and those which were not. Illicit-election tactics can range widely, from the exclusion of candidates, through bribery and intimidation of voters, to simply miscounting the votes. The first question we asked was whether the conduct of the election mattered to its outcome. Unsurprisingly, it did: controlling for other significant influences on the outcome, incumbent political leaders who were able to resort to illicit tactics could expect their subsequent tenure in office to be nearly tripled in duration.

There is thus a strong incentive to cheat. The question becomes what determines whether cheating is feasible. We found that whether elections were clean or dirty could be well explained by a few structural characteristics of a society. Cumulatively, differences in these characteristics produced massive differences in the chances of a fair election. For example, the typical African society has structural characteristics which reduce the chances of a clean election to only around 3 percent, whereas India has characteristics which would give around an 80 percent chance of a clean election. One of the key structural characteristics is the number of checks and balances—again, as measured by veto points. Each veto point substantially increases the chance of a clean election. So, introducing elections in a society before checks and balances have been well-established is asking for trouble. The danger is that the incumbent wins the first election using illicit tactics and then has a strong interest in blocking the establishment of effective checks and balances.

But in regards to the resource curse the key discovery was that resource revenues radically reduced the chance of a clean election. The effect was unfortunately very large. Imagine two hypothetical countries, both of which are absolutely at the global average in every characteristic other than their natural-resource endowment. One of these completely average places, the Boring Republic, has no revenues from natural resources. The other, Boringstan, gets half of its national income from natural resources—a proportion which is high but by no means remarkable. What does our analysis predict about the conduct of elections in these two countries? Elections in the Boring Republic are very likely to be, well, a little boring: there is a 95 percent chance that they will be cleanly conducted. It is the election in Boringstan that is likely to hit the global television screens: there the chances of a clean election drop to only 34 percent. Natural-resource abundance massively erodes the chances of a clean election.

We might wonder whether or not it matters if an election is not properly conducted. In the political sense the answer is too obvious for the question to be worth posing. The whole democratic basis for an election making a government accountable and thereby conferring legitimacy upon it is undermined. But does it matter for the economy?

Recall that Lisa Chauvet and I had investigated whether elections improved economic policy. Our results were encouraging. We found solid evidence that elections disciplined governments into improving important aspects of economic policy. Now it is time for the caveat I mentioned. As in my work with Anke, we distinguished between elections which were clean and those which were badly conducted. It turned out to matter. The disciplining effect of elections only worked when they were fair. Flawed elections had, at best, no beneficial effect on economic policies.

In short, corruption of the electoral process leads to worse economic policies, and is far more likely to happen in a society with abundant natural assets. This may be why we find that in such countries, in the absence of checks and balances, democracy has such disappointing economic consequences.

Finally, return to that question of how to win an election. One of our other results helps to explain why, in countries with clean elections, governments struggle so hard to improve economic policies: good economic performance substantially increases the chances of winning. For example, if during the four years prior to the election the economy has grown at 5 percent instead of stagnating, the duration of the incumbent's term in office is lengthened by 60 percent. In contrast, if the election is not clean the difference made by good economic performance is quite marginal; less than a 20 percent increase in duration. Economic policies can be set so as to reward cronies rather than benefit the broad mass of citizens.

One of the enigmas of development has been Botswana. The country has many features that seem to point to catastrophe: it is a small society and so prone to the dangers of personalized power; it is resource-rich and so prone to patronage politics; it is landlocked and so has few opportunities other than the extraction of its diamonds. Yet Botswana has one of the most successful economies on earth.

A final twist in our results suggests why. Celebrated recent research by Benjamin Jones and Benjamin Olken posed the question: do leaders matter? It concluded that they did. Changes of leaders led to significant changes in economic performance. Anke and I revisited this research, introducing the distinction between clean and dirty elections. We wondered whether fair elections made leaders redundant. Regardless of what leaders would like to do, if they are forced to face a clean election, they have to do their best. We found that the changes of leaders which mattered happened in places in which fraudulent elections enabled those same leaders to pursue the strategy of their personal preference. In such cases it can matter enormously what that preference happens to be. We suspect that the secret of Botswana's success was that its first leaders were dedicated to national success rather than to personal gain. Had they had more self-serving preferences Botswana's institutions were initially unlikely to have been sufficiently strong to block them. Botswana owes a huge debt to those leaders; by the same token, the leaders of those resource-rich societies that have remained mired in poverty, such as Angola, stand condemned. An implication of our work is that the neo-con agenda was naive. For elections to discipline governments into good decisions depends upon a range of institutions that take time to gain trust. Resource-rich countries need good government decisions even more than other societies. But those riches make it more difficult to build the needed institutions. The neo-cons wished an end that was unattainable on their chosen trajectory.

Decisions, Decisions . . .

Where does this leave us? Governance and valuable natural assets become a two-way street. The rents from natural assets corrode governance and potentially this leaves the society worse off than it was without them. But natural assets need good governance in order to be harnessed for the benefit of the society. Tony Venables and I have been trying to model that interaction. Consistent with my earlier empirical results from my work with Benedikt, we find that there can be threshold effects. What matters is the quality of governance relative to the value of the natural assets. Above a certain level the effects of natural assets are mostly benign, lifting the country into prosperity; below, they drag it down.

"Quality of governance" is just fancy language for whether decisions are well-taken and properly implemented. In harnessing depleting natural assets for the wellbeing of ordinary citizens there is no single critical decision; there is a decision chain. You might suppose that the first and overarching decision would be whether to extract the natural asset at all. While this is indeed a decision that has to be taken, the right answer is dependent upon all the others and best left to the end.

The first decision in the chain involves discovering the natural assets that lie under the country's territory. In chapter 4 I will show why it is likely that huge mistakes have been made at this stage. The next decision involves who captures the value of the natural assets that lie beneath the surface of a country. The right answer should be the government. Whether that is what typically happens is the subject of chapter 5. Supposing the government has indeed captured the lion's share of the value, the next decision in the chain concerns the proportion of government revenue that should be consumed as opposed to devoted to acquiring assets. The right answer is that although the society can legitimately consume some of these revenues, divided as it sees fit between public and private consumption, the proportion should be radically lower than that from other sources of government revenue. Whether that is what actually happens is the subject of chapter 6. Supposing the society has consumed only an appropriately modest amount from its resource revenues, the final decision in the chain deals with what it should do with the revenues that it has not consumed. The right choice of assets depends upon the opportunities open to the economy and is the subject of chapter 7. Each of these decisions poses challenges and is distinctive to the management of natural assets. For most wealthy countries natural assets are only a minor component of their overall revenues. In consequence they have not given these decisions much attention. This neglect has had consequences for the bottom billion, for most of which natural assets are far more important.

The prevailing discourse on economic policy in the bottom billion countries is now essentially an echo of that in the rich countries. That problem really struck me only in March 2009 when I was invited to address a meeting of Africa's resource-rich governments. An official from the International Monetary Fund had also been invited to address the meeting. As I listened to her well-crafted PowerPoint presentation I realized that her talk could equally have been delivered to virtually any government audience in the world. Budget deficits should be moderate; the business climate should be conducive to investment; and so forth. There was nothing much wrong with it, but it did not take into account the distinctive nature of the decisions facing a resource-rich, low-income country. Yet each of these decisions poses difficulties. For example, it is easy to say "capture the value of nature assets for the government" but doing it involves technically complex incentive problems. The government can easily so mishandle them that it kills the goose. The politics of capture are equally daunting; it is often more likely that government representatives are captured by private interests, along with the natural assets.

Harnessing natural assets for prosperity depends upon the decision chain. As with a real chain, if any one link is broken the chain as a whole is broken. Harnessing natural assets is therefore a weakest link problem.

The final compounding challenge is that none of these decisions is taken only once. The process by which the extraction of natural assets transforms poverty into prosperity inevitably takes time, typically around a generation. Even if decisions are initially wise, they can be reversed. Plunder looms before the society. The entire decision chain needs to be gotten right again and again.

Each decision is difficult, critical, and reversible, making it all too likely that the extraction of natural assets will not ensure prosperity. The decision to extract should be based on a reasonable judgment about the capacity of the society to get the decision chain right, and to keep it right. There is, I believe, only one way of guaranteeing that, as I will show in the final chapter. But if a reasonable judgment is that the conditions for successful exploitation are not met, then those who participate in the exploitation of natural assets are aiding and abetting plunder. The rightful owners of natural assets are not going to be the beneficiaries. Many criminal acts depend upon a chain of decisions, each decision taking its moral complexion from the whole. Just as the fence who sells stolen goods while turning a blind eye to their origin is implicated in theft, so the moral complexion of resource extraction is determined not by its legality but by its likely beneficiaries.

Forming a judgment as to who the likely beneficiaries will be requires understanding the decision chain. We will take it link by link.

CHAPTER 4

Discovering Natural Assets

NATURAL ASSETS ARE LIVING DANGEROUSLY: lacking natural owners they are liable to be plundered. Since mankind has had a long time in which to plunder, those depleting natural assets that are still around are there because they are difficult to extract. They lie beneath the earth, hence why they are called "subsoil assets." Where are they?

The Planet in Quadrants

The world currently consists of 194 nation states, which can conveniently be grouped, as we've seen, into four roughly equal quadrants: the rich countries of the OECD; the countries of the bottom billion; Russia and China with their satellites; and the emerging market economies, such as India and Brazil. Each group occupies around a quarter of the planet's land surface area.

Occasionally national borders have been determined by the presence of subsoil assets. British colonial pioneers, for example, got wind of the existence of deposits of copper in central Africa and so pushed a railway line northward from South Africa. They found the copper belt in what is now Zambia. Having pushed over two thousand miles, however, they missed by some thirty the far richer copper deposits that now lie in the southeast corner of the Democratic Republic of the Congo. But usually, national borders do not reflect the endowments of subsoil assets to any significant degree. It would therefore be reasonable to regard subsoil assets as being randomly distributed between countries.

Further, countries in the four groups are scattered across the planet. Although each group adds up to around a quarter of the planet's total land area, it does not literally make up a quadrant, a neat quarter-slice out of a global orange. Since subsoil assets are randomly distributed among the 194 countries, and each of the four groups of countries is fairly randomly distributed around the earth, we might expect the law of large numbers to even out the distribution of subsoil assets among the groups. That is, while the random distribution over the 194 countries is likely to produce some spectacular differences between lucky and unlucky countries, by the time we have aggregated them into four massive groups the remaining differences should be much smaller.

A possible qualification would arise if an unusual abundance of natural assets made it more likely that a society would belong to one or other of the four groups. If abundance automatically enabled rapid development, the rich countries would tend to have more subsoil assets; while if abundance was generally an impediment to development we would expect the bottom billion nations to have more. As I argued in the previous chapter, the evidence suggests that the endowment of natural assets has ambiguous effects, which depend upon the initially prevailing level of governance. So we would not expect the extreme endowments to cluster—the countries with natural abundance all being in the OECD and the countries with nothing all among the bottom billion, or the other way around. If anything, given the difficulty of harnessing natural assets, we might even expect that the resource-abundant countries would end up disproportionately in the bottom billion. In consequence, the quadrant of the bottom billion should tend to have more natural assets than the OECD quadrant.

There is another reason why we might expect to find such a pattern: the countries of the OECD have been extracting their subsoil assets for industrialization for the past two centuries whereas in the bottom billion extraction only got underway recently. For example, Britain has exhausted most of the coal that it began to mine in the nineteenth century and most of the oil that it discovered in the 1960s. There should therefore be more natural assets left in the bottom billion than in the rich countries, which industrialized on the back of depletable resources. These expectations are indeed consistent with the perception that most of the societies of the bottom billion are resource-rich: the poor world has nature and the rich world has industry.

I've mentioned that for the millennium the World Bank produced a global snapshot of subsoil assets, country by country. Anke and I reorganized the data so that for each country it showed the average subsoil assets per square kilometer. We started by taking the quadrant of the rich-country club, the OECD. The value of subsoil assets as of the millennium was $114,000 per average square kilometer of land in this quarter of the planet. So, even after two centuries of extraction there is fortunately still quite a lot left to exploit.

Armed with the figure of $114,000 for the typical square kilometer in the rich world, we then turned to Africa and the other countries of the bottom billion. The magazine image of Africa is that it is superabundant in natural assets; the big-picture view of global economic development during this century is that Africa will export its abundance of natural resources as inputs to Asian industry. Indeed, we might expect Africa to be particularly endowed with natural assets because although there have been some terrible historical instances of plunder, the extraction of Africa's subsoil assets started much more recently than in the rich world. In my recent lectures I have challenged the audience to vote on whether Africa has more or less subsoil assets per square kilometer than the rich world. The voting is running about 99–1 in favor of more. Yet the average square kilometer of Africa has only $23,000 of subsoil assets. The truth is that Africa is actually strikingly poor in subsoil assets. It only seems rich in natural assets because it lacks other assets: relative to its man-made assets it indeed has an abundance of natural assets. Africa is even lacking in subsoil assets relative to the countries of the bottom billion in Asia and South America; the average for the entire group is $29,000, still way below that for the OECD.

The question becomes why the bottom billion countries are so much less endowed with subsoil assets than the rich. Like the rich world they form a truly enormous land mass. Simply from the perspective of statistical chance we would not expect two very large, geologically random quarters of the planet to display such a large difference. But what was being measured in that World Bank snapshot was not a country's endowment of subsoil assets; rather it was its *known* endowment. Those natural assets that have not been discovered could not, of course, be included in a valuation: of that which we cannot speak, we must perforce be silent, (or did someone else say that?)

There are two distinct possible explanations for the stark difference. One is that the countries of the bottom billion have been uncommonly unlucky. Were we to take that line of analysis, we might conclude that one reason the rich world is rich is that it was lucky in its endowments of natural assets. The other explanation is that the countries of the bottom billion have as much, if not more, natural assets under their soil, but have not searched for them. One way to distinguish is to look at the evidence on search. For example, in areas that are geologically possible candidates for oil, we can count the density of drilling. There has been far less drilling in the bottom billion than in the rich world.

That the explanation for the apparent shortfall in subsoil assets is lack of prospecting seems to me most likely. Indeed, I would say that the assumption of similar endowments of subsoil assets is in fact conservative. The much shorter history of extraction by itself should imply that considerably more is still there, waiting to be extracted.

If the countries of the bottom billion have only around a quarter as much of the known endowment of the rich countries because the other three-quarters have not yet been found, this has three major implications. One, which is the overarching theme of this book, is that the natural assets of the bottom billion constitute a massive opportunity. They are sufficiently valuable that, properly harnessed, they could be transformative. Already Africa's revenues from natural assets dwarf both aid and other sources of income. In 2008 Angola alone received from oil more than double the entire aid flows to all the countries of the bottom billion. Multiply these revenues by four to bring them up to likely equivalence with the OECD. Of course even the OECD countries have by no means completed the prospecting of their territory. Prospecting is expensive and improvements in the technology of search periodically make new prospecting worthwhile. Further, technical progress periodically confers value on minerals that were previously not worth extracting. A four-fold increase in the known subsoil assets of the bottom billion is merely the lower bound to the true value of what is waiting to be discovered.

A second implication is that from now on global discoveries of natural resources will be located disproportionately in the politically difficult territories of the bottom billion: the easier resources have already been discovered. The discovery process in the bottom billion will be of global significance for future supply of essential materials. This shift is already underway. In 2000 only 7 percent of the world's oil came from the bottom billion; by 2008 it was over 10 percent.

It is the third implication that I want to pursue here: if the countries of the bottom billion have discovered only around a quarter as many of its natural assets as the rich world, then something must have gone pretty drastically wrong with the discovery process.

Dilemmas of Discovery

So how should that discovery process be managed? The outcomes to be avoided are at one extreme a long period of neglect, and at the other, a gold rush. With current technology, finding out precisely what is under the ground is very expensive. Perhaps advances in technology will make the search process cheaper. This in turn may be a good reason for not trying to gather complete information about the subsoil assets of an entire country all at once. Gold rushes happen because information is a public good: the first strike provides useful information to others. In economics such effects are known as "externalities": benefits that accrue inadvertently from the actions of one person to other people.

Externalities sound nice, but they are a problem. The person taking the initial action couldn't care less about the benefits that might accrue to others whereas a socially beneficial decision should take them into account. The challenge of how to get such benefits taken into account is described by economists as internalizing the externalities into the decision process, and there are two ways to do it. Both involve creating a monopoly. The first creates a private monopoly. The government could, for example, sell the exclusive rights to prospecting anywhere in the country to a single company. Since the prospecting process may last for decades, so would the exclusive rights. The alternative is for the government itself to do the prospecting. It might do this either directly or by hiring a company to survey the country's geology.

In special circumstances these two approaches might achieve the same benign outcome. A large private corporation might be prepared to pay the government for the exclusive long-term rights of prospecting precisely the value that might be expected had the government done the prospecting itself. But under normal circumstances this approach is a bad deal for the society. An analogy would be the basic scientific research on the foundations of which more practical discoveries are built. Again, this basic scientific research is replete with externalities, so one approach would be to award a monopoly to a single company. But in practice, much of the research is funded by the government or foundations, rather than by for-profit companies. By the same reasoning, it is usually appropriate for the initial geological surveys to be publicly funded. Such surveys reveal the potential for more localized search.

The remaining unexplored parts of the world's geology are largely in the countries of the bottom billion: places like Sierra Leone, Liberia and the Democratic Republic of the Congo. Think why a commercial company is liable to under-pay for the right to say a century-long monopoly of prospecting rights in such a country.

The most obvious reason is corruption. The company is negotiating with a person, or a small group, whose responsibility it is to represent the interests of citizens, both living and yet to be born. Although the job of those representatives is to safeguard the public interest, they also have individual private interests, and ordinary citizens may have little control over them. Citizens may not be able to scrutinize deals, and even if one appears to be suspect they may have no effective recourse. Knowing this, companies have an incentive to offer bribes, and representatives have an incentive to accept them. The amount of money at stake is so enormous and the effective scrutiny so limited that any other type of behavior would be quixotic. Corruption benefits the public officials who negotiate the deal and the company that bribes them; it underpays. Both come at the expense of ordinary citizens.

A slightly less obvious reason is what economists call asymmetric information. If you do not understand what that term means, then we have an example of it: I know something that you don't. Suppose that Global Copper Incorporated sits down at a negotiating table with a minister from the government of Guinea Bissau. Global Copper Incorporated has years of accumulated experience in copper prospecting, has already hired the best experts on earth to estimate the probabilities of finds of various values, and work out profitability over the likely range of future prices of copper. The government of Guinea Bissau has no experience of copper mining. Perhaps it has hired an international law firm, which will do its best to alert the government to contract clauses that might look innocuous yet turn out to be treacherous. Who do you imagine knows more about the likely value of the rights to prospecting for copper in the country over the next century? Asymmetric information is likely to lead to the more informed party benefiting at the expense of the less informed party. The result is always the same: the company underpays.

An even less obvious but far more important reason involves what economists call "time-inconsistency," which arises when a government cannot make a credible commitment on a deal. Governments are sovereign and so face major difficulties in legally committing themselves. Any contract that the government enters into can be torn up in its own courts. If the company is astute it will recognize that the proffered deal is too good to last. Let us pay Global Copper Incorporated the courtesy of assuming that its senior management is not stupid. In this case it would be the government that loses out as a result of the time-consistency problem. No company is fool enough to enter into deals that, however potentially mutually beneficial, are going to get broken. As a result, the government loses its share of these potential benefits. By trying to snatch the cream, it loses the milk. The most spectacularly time-inconsistent prospecting deal I have come across was that struck by Columbus with the Spanish crown. By the time he sailed into the ocean blue he and his descendants were legally entitled to one quarter of whatever was found in any lands discovered on his voyages in perpetuity. Columbus duly went off and found the Americas. Sure enough the Spanish crown reneged. But then, Columbus was probably not as savvy as Global Copper Incorporated.

The time-consistency problem will reappear in the next chapter, where I discuss devising a tax system on the extraction of a subsoil asset that has already been discovered. Sovereignty does not disappear, and so the time-consistency problem does not go away. But once the subsoil asset has been discovered it is far less acute. There is a key difference between selling the rights for the extraction of known resources and selling the rights for prospecting: the element of luck. Of course it is not possible to eliminate luck from business. But with prospecting for a valuable natural asset the outcomes are essentially bimodal: either nothing of value is found, or a sufficient amount is found to make the enterprise highly profitable. The intermediate outcome of finding just enough to make a normal return on the capital invested, which is the most likely outcome with many other investments, is highly unlikely in prospecting. This bimodality intensifies the time-inconsistency problem.

The problem arises where the government has an incentive to promise something to a private company like Global Copper but then renege once the company has made some irreversible decision. Suppose that so little is known about the geology of a region that there is a 90 percent chance of finding nothing, and a 10 percent chance of finding natural assets the extraction of which will generate a surplus of $5 billion over and above the costs of extraction. From these numbers the economists at Global Copper will calculate something termed the "expected value," which is merely the sum of each outcome multiplied by the probability of its occurrence. The expected value of prospecting is $500 million: 10 percent of $5 billion. Suppose that the costs of prospecting are $200 million. These costs are upfront and cannot be recovered if nothing is found; a mineshaft to nothing is of no value to anyone. So, in principle, the company should be willing to pay the government around $300 million for the rights to prospecting: representing the expected value from prospecting minus the costs of undertaking the search. The government can structure these payments of $300 million in various ways, but let's keep things simple and suppose that it decides to stack it all onto a single upfront payment. It promises a tax-free environment, and hopes to get all the $300 million at the point of signature, which is called a "signature bonus."

Why might the company hesitate to hand over anything like $300 million for these rights? Because there are only two outcomes: if the company finds nothing then, bad luck, it has lost $200 million spent on sinking a mine to nowhere: well, that's business. But suppose it strikes lucky: it stands to make $5 billion on extracting natural assets. The government now has a huge incentive to renege on its promise: the company is making $4,500 million more than it spent: even if it pulls out the government can resell the extraction rights to some other company for around that figure. Perhaps the government feels honor-bound to stick to the commitment, but in that eventuality an opposition party is likely to accuse the government of having thrown away the country's valuable natural assets for peanuts. After all, the company only paid $300 million for something which is worth $4.8 billion.

The board of Global Copper runs through these scenarios and recognizes that the promise of zero taxation is time-inconsistent. It will react by heavily discounting what it is willing to pay for the rights to search. Is the problem simply caused by the government's attempt to stack everything onto the signature bonus? Suppose that instead at the time of prospecting it had proffered a tax system that generated revenue over the course of extraction. Now the company only has to pay the government money if and when it actually strikes copper. Nevertheless, the proffered tax regime would still need to leave the company with enough profits to cover the costs of prospecting. But the costs of prospecting—the $200 million—are certain, whereas profits only accrue with a 10 percent chance of success, so the tax regime must leave the company with $2 billion profit to cover it. Should the company strike it lucky it is still in clover; the $200 million it spent on prospecting is still dwarfed by the $2 billion it receives in post-tax copper revenues. That $2 billion, however, is politically too vulnerable to be counted on.

Of course I made the above numbers up. But in the brief time between writing the text and correcting the proofs, a dispute between

Kosmos Oil and the government of Ghana reproduced them in real life. The time-consistency problem is not just a hypothesis.

Search as a Public Good

So, where have we got to in the search problem? The public good nature of the search process makes it efficient to internalize externalities by having a single entity undertake the search. One way of doing this would be for the government to sell extraction rights to any natural assets found to a monopoly. But the time-consistency problem kills that idea. Prospecting is generally said to be too risky for its costs to be borne by the government of a low-income country; better for foreign enterprise to bear them. The fallacy in that analysis is that a substantial part of the risks of prospecting are not geological, but political: the government itself is the unknown that the company has to take into account, discounting what the search rights are worth by the risk that the government will renege on its commitments. Obviously, if the government itself finances the search costs it does not bear these risks and so it is more cost-effective. This does not imply that the government should itself run the prospecting process. The typical government of the bottom billion is drastically short of management capacity and prospecting is a highly skilled and specialized activity. The search process should be contracted out to reputable companies hired to produce a geological survey.

Once the government has secured reliable geological information it can then make it available as a public good. Such information cannot produce guarantees, but it can considerably shorten the odds on subsequent prospecting. If the search odds are not 1-in-10 but 1-in-2, the severity of the time-consistency problem is diminished. If it strikes it rich Global Copper still does well, of course, but the ratio of cost to gain no longer looks obscene and its license to prospect is therefore far less subject to being torn up by an opportunistic future government.

The geological information thus not only clarifies what the rights to extraction are worth in each specific location, but reduces the political risk. Further, by diminishing the uncertainty from prospecting it reduces the externalities from individual search plot-by-plot. Remember, it was these externalities that made it more profitable for the government to sell the search rights as a national monopoly rather than plot-by-plot. A major advantage of selling the rights off plot-by-plot is that not all the extraction rights need be sold at the same time. A government can thereby control the pace at which the country's natural assets are extracted. Phasing their sale has a further advantage: to the extent that discoveries on one plot still confer useful information as to what is likely to be found in other plots, phasing the sale of plots gradually reduces the uncertainty as to the value of plots and this will tend to raise the price that companies are willing to pay for them. By phasing search the government ensures that more geological information becomes public and so enhances the value of the remaining sales.

Nevertheless, it might be advantageous for the government to package the rights into quite large units; plots may need to be big to be attractive. This is because the technology of mining usually favors scale: the bigger the mine, the less the per-unit cost of natural assets extracted. This became apparent during the gold rush in South Africa. The government sold off plots in tiny units, perhaps thinking that this would raise the most money. But in order to bring the gold to the surface each tiny plot had to sink its own narrow mineshaft. Cecil Rhodes was the first to realize that if these little miners were consolidated scale economies would lower the costs of extraction and make the rights more valuable. The scale economies led all the way to monopoly: by the time he had finished consolidating the industry, Rhodes's company, De Beers, owned every single mine. But much of the value of the rights accrued to the consolidator rather than to the government, which had sold the rights in units that were too small.

Because search is, nevertheless, high risk, it is ideally financed by aid. Donors are better placed to bear these risks than are governments. A major donor such as the World Bank can average out the risk by funding prospecting in many of the countries of the bottom billion. A one-in-ten risk country by country shrinks to a negligible overall risk if undertaken in ten countries.

In the bottom billion basic prospecting should be undertaken as a public good, and it should be financed predominantly by donors. This is not what actually happens; far from it. For example, in Zambia, government geologists told me that the most recent public information on the country's natural assets dates from the 1950s. There has never been a mineral discovery in the country farther than ten miles from a major road. I recently addressed an international conference on the extractive industries attended by many of the major companies. When I suggested that basic prospecting should be done before companies were offered the extraction rights my proposal was greeted by a combination of derision and horror. Perhaps I misunderstood something fundamental; I do not discount this possibility. But perhaps the companies realized the implications and did not like them.

As to donors financing public prospecting, to date they have preferred spending their money on more photogenic expenditures, such as a village school or a rural clinic. Were a donor to finance the cost of a geological survey it might well be criticized by an alliance of the compassion NGOs and the environmental NGOs—a prospect sufficient to scare off most development agencies. Yet precisely because prospecting is high-risk, it is likely to have a high return. Currently, to my knowledge, only the Chinese are offering to finance geological surveys for free.

So much for that first link in the decision chain: discovering what natural assets are there to be extracted. It is not a link to which much thought has been given yet the mistakes that have been made are truly massive. In sheer quantitative terms the key problem for the bottom billion is not that their natural assets have been plundered. Rather, it is that they have not yet been discovered.

CHAPTER 5

Capturing Natural Assets

ONCE NATURAL ASSETS HAVE BEEN DISCOVERED comes the second link in the decision chain: how their value should be captured by society. "Captured by society" means that the value of natural assets should accrue as revenue to government, the representative of society.

In the bottom billion there is often a gulf between what should happen and what actually does happen. The value of natural assets is captured, but not always by government. Sometimes we find plunder in its crudest form, as for example when a corrupt minister strikes a deal with a shady resource-extraction company. The minister gets handsomely rewarded and deposits his share of the profits in a foreign bank account. The company makes a fortune, which benefits its shareholders, none of whom are citizens of the country from which the natural assets have been removed.

Underlying stories such as this are two distinct problems. The most obvious is corruption, just as at the prospecting stage. The interests of the country and its citizens are necessarily represented by its government, and indeed, not by its entire government but by a handful of people: perhaps the president, the minister of mines, and a couple of high officials. The resource-extraction company bribes these representatives, inducing them to ignore their professional responsibilities in favor of their personal interests. Bribes are, of course, never termed "bribes"; they are "facilitation payments," often made by the resource-extraction company to local companies for unspecified services and whose beneficial ownership is opaque.

Countering Corruption

There are two defenses against corruption: transparency and an effective legal system. Because governments are one of the parties to corruption, they are often reluctant to permit transparency and generate criminal investigations. Fortunately, however, each of them can be reinforced internationally.

The Publish What You Pay campaign pressures resource-extraction companies into releasing information on the payments that they are making to governments. The idea is that once these payments become public knowledge it is much more difficult for corrupt officials and politicians to siphon off the money. Citizens match the money paid by companies to income entered on the official rolls. Once the money is placed into the government budget parliaments can follow it; whereas until it enters the budget there is no process of oversight. The campaign began as a small NGO but has now evolved into an international organization: the Extractive Industries Transparency Initiative.

Transparency is by no means enough to prevent corruption, but without it plunder is all too likely. A couple of years ago I was invited to the Cameroons to address a gathering of African officials on the management of natural assets. As is common with such events, the meeting was opened by the president, who was showered with effusive praise for his valiant efforts over the years to develop his country. The hotel in which the meeting was held was certainly very fine, by repute the finest in the country. I noticed, however, that it did not have Internet coverage. At the end of the conference I drove from the capital, Yaoundé, to the port city of Doula. This was the main transport artery not only for the Cameroons but also for the landlocked Central African Republic. By the end of my journey I had concluded that whatever the president had spent the oil money on, it had gone neither into telecoms nor roads, as important as these are for development. In 2009 Albert Zeufack, an Ivorian economist, and Bernard Gauthier, a Canadian, produced a study on what had happened to Cameroon's oil revenues. The study was pioneering because there was virtually no official data on either how much money had come in or on how it had been used. However, they did a brilliant job of piecing it together. Combining production data recently released as part of the Transparency Initiative with cost and price data from a range of sources, they estimated approximately what revenues must have been. They then compared these estimates with the revenues officially reported in the budget.

The president had kept the oil money well away from the budget. Indeed, until 1986 he had kept much of it well away from the country, placing it in secret foreign accounts. At the time this had been praised by the World Bank as prudent, keeping the money hidden reduced domestic pressures to spend it. When oil prices crashed in 1986, the president indeed brought some of the money back into the country to sustain recurrent spending. But much of it never returned and disappeared without trace. What did not happen, either then or ever since, was investment within the country: what I saw—or didn't see—was the tip of an iceberg.

So, transparency matters. Currently, the government of Cameroon is signed up to the principles of the Extractive Industries Transparency Initiative. These principles include a requirement the government release audited accounts, showing what it has received. Or at least, that is what the English version of the EITI principles says. Unfortunately, the French version at one key point is ambiguous, and the government has chosen to interpret the ambiguity as absolving it of the responsibility of having to release the relevant information. Albert and Bernard investigated whether, since the government had signed the EITI commitment, the share of oil payments accruing to the budget has increased, and concluded that to date it has not. The battle over transparency is not yet won.

The other international defense against bribery is if the governments of the countries which are the home to the resource-extraction companies punish it. If companies did not offer bribes, government officials could not divert money from the public purse to their private pockets. Only recently have bribes by these companies headquartered in the rich countries become illegal. No government wanted to take the lead and thereby disadvantage its companies. Eventually, this problem was overcome by the OECD, which organized a common change in national laws. However, making something illegal is one thing, actually bringing prosecution is another. Some governments, notably Britain, have to date simply not bothered to enforce the new laws. I have just been asked by Britain's Serious Fraud Office to be an expert witness in the first-ever prosecution. For obvious reasons I cannot go into most of the details of the case; but one detail is truly revealing. It demonstrates why bribery can be crushingly damaging for a society. The person who received the bribes, which went on for a period of years, was initially a middle-ranking government bureaucrat. But the bribes were sufficiently large to enable him to embark upon a political career. In due course he was elected to his country's parliament (refer back to chapter 3 to see how money might help win an election). But by the time that the bribes came to light he had risen further: he was a prominent government minister, in charge of policy for an economically vital sector. The cost of bribes is not the money spent on the bribe; it is the corrosive effect it has on the selection of politicians. Those bribes may have displaced an honest person from office, someone who would have set policies for the national interest instead of for personal gain.

Leveling the Playing Field

That seemingly simple example of a corrupt official being bribed by a foreign company contained a second and more subtle type of problem. The corrupt minister was probably himself being ripped off by the company because he was on the wrong end of the asymmetric information problem that I introduced in the previous chapter. He simply did not know as much as the company offering the bribes about the true value of the contracts he was awarding.

There is an institutional technology for overcoming the asymmetric information problem: selling the extraction rights through auction. Auctions can be complicated, but they can level the playing field between a savvy company and an ignorant government. The key is to get several companies to bid against each other. The rule of thumb seems to be that you need around four of them. If it is just between, say, Global Copper Incorporated and Allied Copper there is too great a risk that they will quietly do a deal: Global agrees to bid low on this one and in return Allied bids low on the next. At the other extreme, if twenty companies all bid, the chances of any one of them winning are too low to justify serious upfront expenditure on the information needed for an accurate estimate of the value of the rights. If every company is buying a pig in a poke they will all bid low; one of them will be lucky but the government will come out badly. Although auctions can go wrong, done right the competition between similarly well-informed bidders inadvertently reveals the true value, regardless of how little the government itself knows.

Here is some telling evidence as to their efficacy. In 2000 the British Treasury decided to sell rights, which it recognized to be very valuable. These were not for natural assets, however; they were for the mobile-phone network. But for our purposes the difference is immaterial. The Treasury, with the full panoply of its expertise, decided to negotiate a deal with a telecoms company and worked out that the right price should be £2 billion (roughly $3.5 billion). Fortunately for British taxpayers, at the last minute some economists succeeded in persuading the Treasury that even with all its magisterial expertise it might be on the wrong side of the asymmetric information problem. In other words the British Treasury might be clueless. For once the Treasury took the advice of economists and sold the rights by auction. They fetched not £2 billion but £20 billion. I ask my friends in African governments, if with all its awesome expertise the British Treasury can be out by a factor of ten, what can they expect of their own ministries of finance when they negotiate deals for the sale of prospecting rights? The day after I had put this to the President of Sierra Leone he telephoned the World Bank for advice on how to run an auction.

But a government should not literally sell all the rights to the natural asset in an auction. It should retain a considerable interest in its assets through the future taxation of company revenues from extraction. But if the government is free to set any tax rates that it chooses, what has the company bought: only the right to generate revenues that might then be entirely taxed away? Such rights would not be worth much. It is not enough to run a good auction. A company needs to know exactly what the tax rules will be before it can decide how much it is willing to bid.

Tax Dilemmas

A tax system can be badly designed in various respects. One is that it gives a company an incentive to reduce its tax bill by reducing overall pre-tax profitability, introducing inefficiency. Another is that it can shift too much risk onto the government, which might get huge revenues at times when global commodity prices are high and nothing when they are low. The government may be unable to handle such wild swings in its revenues. Yet another is that it simply leaves too much profit with the company. If extraction rights are being auctioned, it might appear not to matter if too much profit is left with the company: low taxation would be offset by willingness on the part of companies to pay a higher upfront price. Yet usually a promise of low taxation is a problem; the time-consistency problem again rears its head. It is one thing for a government to promise low taxation and another for it to stick to that promise. The calculus of advantage for the government changes once the company has invested in, for example, sinking the mine. Even if it made good commercial sense for the government to *make* a commitment, it is unlikely to make good sense for it to *honor* that commitment. Once the company has made an irreversible investment it is a sunk cost. It will still have an incentive to operate the mine even if the government reneges on its agreement and imposes higher taxes. Indeed, the company has little recourse. Knowing all this in advance, it will not bid sufficiently high to offset a low-tax commitment.

The government can reduce the time-consistency problem—although not eliminate it—by announcing in advance of the auction that it will capture most of the asset revenues from tax receipts rather than from the auction price. It should try to lock itself in to such a tax structure through legal means to the extent possible, but it will be much more credible if it is designed so as to avoid major inefficiencies and to allow for contingencies.

The most obvious contingency is that the world price of the commodity is likely to change. Commodity prices are hugely volatile and even their long-term average is unpredictable. If all the risk is borne by the company it may end up with a deal that is too good to be true. Precisely this happened recently in Zambia. At the time when world copper prices were at a historic low, the international company that owned the main copper mine, Anglo-American, decided to pull out. Since the closure of the mines would have had politically devastating consequences for employment, it was imperative for the government either to re-nationalize them or to find a new buyer. The government knew that the best chance of a return to profitability was if a huge investment was made in opening deposits of ore, which required a very deep mine. There was no way that the state could finance this investment, so it had to attract a foreign company. It therefore set tax rates on copper extraction very low. This was sensible, and a company stepped in, except that the Zambian government and its advisors forgot to consider that copper mining might become very profitable again if the world price of copper jumped sufficiently. No provision was made in the contract for such an eventuality. Instead, low taxes were promised for the next fifteen years without any contingencies—perhaps both the government and the company regarded rising prices as too unlikely to worry about.

Within five years of signing the contract, however, the world copper price had started to soar. By 2008 it had reached an all-time high that generated huge profits for the company. As a result of the tax commitment the government itself received virtually nothing from the copper boom: on a base of copper exports of around $2 billion, tax revenues from the copper companies amounted to merely $30 million, and even this exaggerated the net receipts because the taxes were offset by a special subsidy they received on electricity. The World Bank estimated that had Zambia had the same tax regime as the other major copper exporter, Chile, its annual revenue would have been around $800 million.

In this situation it seemed to me that the case for renegotiating the contract was overwhelming: the design of the original contract had been very badly flawed. Whether renegotiation was wise was hotly contested: when I broached the matter both with the Zambian government and with staff of the international agencies their response was that the government needed to protect its reputation. My own view was that the reputation of the government of Zambia was not worth $770 million per year, but worried that I might be wrong I took the issue up the hierarchy of the agency to very senior management. I remember being ushered into the football-field sized office, along with the country team. The official listened to the numbers and scribbled something on a scrap of paper. "They don't need an economist," he said, with a contemptuous sweep of the eyes that took in both me and his staff. "They need a lawyer." I felt vindicated, but the story ended badly. The government did renegotiate: a messy and protracted process which indeed cost it its reputation. But the very month in which the new tax regime came into effect the global economic crisis struck and the world copper price collapsed. The companies promptly pressured the government into scrapping the main new tax. The story did not end there: within months the world price of copper rose again. This is where the situation rests at the time of writing: low taxation and a high copper price.

In retrospect, the key lesson was that a tax structure should build in contingencies. Changes in global prices are not just a possibility, they are a certainty. Further, their implications for profitability are easy enough to calculate and so there is no excuse for not building them in to the original terms of the tax regime.

Unfortunately, we are not done with the problems of corruption and asymmetric information. They reappear in a dispute between specialists that might seem arcane but is in fact quite straightforward. It is whether revenues should be raised by means of "excess" profits taxes or royalties. Compare a manufacturing company with a resource-extraction company. Both make profits, but those of the manufacturing company are a return on its investment and the risks it takes. The profits of the resource-extraction company are partly also a return on investment and risk, but on top of these it is benefiting from the natural assets which it sells. In some cases both the costs of extraction and the risks will be minimal, while the natural assets might be worth a fortune, so that most of the company's profit is really just the sale of assets that belong to citizens: this is the excess profit. Economists confine the term "profit" to the return on capital and risk: anything over and above that is "rent." The rents on natural assets differ: most of the value of a barrel of oil is rent, whereas most of the value of a ton of coal is a return on the capital and labor used in its extraction.

If the tax authorities and the company have precisely the same information, the ideal approach is to tax ordinary profits at the same rate as those of manufacturing companies—say 30 percent—while taxing the excess profits, or rents, at 99 percent. By their nature, rents are not a return on either capital or risk, so the company does not need to be rewarded for generating them. So applied, an excess-profits tax can reach the parts that a royalty cannot reach. A "royalty" is a much cruder device: payments are tied to gross revenues rather than to net profits and this introduces inefficiency. But the superiority of profits taxes is dependent upon that opening caveat: the tax authorities need *the same information* as the company. That can be rather a substantial caveat because we are likely to be in a world of extreme asymmetric information: the company can accurately distinguish between its profits and its rents, but not the tax authorities. As an employee in the Zambian Revenue Authority put it to me with disarming honesty, "The companies have all the best accountants." Negotiating from superior knowledge, companies can often end up with tax agreements that are decidedly advantageous. Mongolia is currently exporting several hundred million dollars worth of gold. The company mining the gold explained to the government the high investment costs of extraction and, while agreeing to a reasonable tax schedule, proposed an initial tax holiday. Having been granted a tax holiday of eight years, the company vigorously set about extracting the gold: it will be exhausted in seven years.

Now add in the problem of corruption: which in this context means that the company has an incentive to cheat. Royalties have one important advantage over excess profits taxes: gross revenues are much more observable to the tax authorities than net profits. This is not merely hypothetical. In 2006 the Chilean government, which has the reputation of being highly astute, switched from an excess-profits tax on copper to a royalty. It did so because in all the years that it had been imposing a profits tax not a single cent had been raised. Somehow, the copper companies kept failing to make any net profits: large revenues were always offset by large expenses.

Information asymmetries and corruption may have found their apogee in the Democratic Republic of the Congo. In October 2009 the *Financial Times* reported that out of gold exports estimated to be around a billion dollars, the government was capturing revenues of only $37,000. When I raised the issue with the Minister of Finance he doubted the accuracy of the numbers but agreed that there was a massive problem of smuggling.

The information asymmetry between tax authorities and a company can be narrowed if the authorities hire specialist accountancy firms to audit the company's books. When the government of Nigeria belatedly did this in 2004 it received a large windfall back-payment. It is a matter of finding the right trade-off between different types of problems: personally I think that a realistic tax regime is likely to include a royalty.

So, where have we got to? A sensible approach is to design a tax structure which has the obvious contingencies built into it, and based on those aspects of a company's activities that are readily observable, but which does not sacrifice too much by way of inefficiency. The government should then try to commit to it. However the key to credibility will be whether the system can adjust to a wide range of circumstances. Once the tax regime is in place the government conducts an auction that reflects whatever dimension it most cares about. That dimension could, of course, be money and often is. Companies are asked to state how much they will pay upfront for the exclusive right to extract natural assets from a particular plot. These amounts are the signature bonuses. Done properly they make sense for cash-starved governments, which get an early injection of money some years before a mine starts to generate tax revenues. But the bidding does not necessarily have to revolve around money. It might be about how many local jobs an extraction company will generate.

Two key principles ought to determine the logic behind the bidding. One is that whatever is included be readily observable and enforceable. Signature bonuses have an advantage here because if the company does not pay it the government does not sign the contract. Employment commitments are much more problematic. Often the government has no means for measuring them and so the company may be tempted to promise more than it intends to deliver. The other principle is that should the bidding involve more than one dimension, the "weights" applied to each dimension—that is, their relative importance—must be clear in advance. Otherwise, it is too easy for the auction to be corrupted. One of the bidding companies might bribe an official and offer a lot on one of the dimensions, while offering little on the others; the official then manipulates the weights so that this company wins.

Signature bonuses can be useful, but they can also be a menace. Obviously, the lower the taxes imposed the more that can be raised from the signature bonus. This can tempt a government into snatching money now at the expense of money later. The sort of government most likely to be tempted by this does not care much about planning ahead. Signature bonuses can thus facilitate plunder of the future by dishonest or short-sighted officials.

By the turn of the millennium the scandals of past resource extraction were so apparent that they had created momentum for reform. The system that I have sketched—by which natural assets would accrue to citizens by means of revenues flowing into the government budget—looked as though it would gradually be adopted over the ensuing decade. Instead, there followed an unprecedented global commodity boom and what might be called the Scramble for Africa Mark II. The Scramble for Africa Mark I, otherwise known as colonialism, had been between the various European imperial powers over the continent's natural assets. The Scramble for Africa Mark II was over those same assets, but predominantly between Asia and North America.

In this second Scramble China avoided head-to-head competition by offering a new type of deal: it would build infrastructure in return for extraction rights. In fact, such deals were not entirely new: in the 1970s European governments had sometimes negotiated such deals. But by the time that the Chinese were doing it this sort of deal had been squeezed out of their repertoire as insufficiently transparent: European and American resource-extraction companies were now offering money. The Chinese offers of infrastructure and the monetary offers of the European and American companies could potentially have been made commensurate, but this did not happen. In the Chinese deals extraction rights were sold discreetly, without direct competition.

Since neither the infrastructure nor the extraction rights involved in the offers were given an explicit monetary value it was hard to see whether these were highly advantageous for Africa, or highly advantageous for China. The response of the international agencies to the Chinese approach was to condemn them: the deals should be unbundled into a monetary payment for the rights to extract resources, and a monetary payment by the African government for infrastructure. That way the deals would be open to international competition, ensuring fair value. The Chinese deals, negotiated in secrecy, had the potential to create all the problems we have encountered: corruption, asymmetric information, and time-inconsistency. However, finger-wagging at China has met with the predictable response. By 2008 the EITI executive was sufficiently concerned to ask me to suggest an alternative approach, one I will outline in the next chapter.

Why Not Nationalize Resource Extraction?

If resource-extraction companies have ripped off governments through a cocktail of corruption, asymmetric information, and discounts that reflect the time-consistency problem, and if prospecting is in any case best financed by government, why not let government handle the exploitation of natural assets? Why not run natural assets through state-owned companies? I can sense a frisson of horror running through my fellow economists: governments should not get directly involved in running economic activities.

In practice, several governments do run resource-extraction businesses. Although in recent decades conventional economic wisdom has been to get government out of such activities, in fact the record is not uniformly bad. The Norwegian government, which can be held up as a model of how to manage a national asset for the benefit of ordinary citizens, established a government-owned oil company as soon as oil was discovered, and gave it a central role in exploitation. One advantage was that the government gradually built up know-how on the business of extracting oil from under the North Sea, and this virtually eliminated the asymmetric information problem. *Ah well*, you may be thinking, *that was Norway; developing countries are different*. Yet Malaysia took the same decision and has fared equally well. Its national company is now a major player in oil exploration around the world, able to compete successfully with the private sector companies. Nowadays Malaysia is a highly successful middle-income country; at the time it established the state-owned oil company it was poor and struggling.

Nevertheless, the more common record of state-owned natural-resource companies has indeed ranged from poor to catastrophic. Across the Strait of Malacca from Malaysia, Indonesia established a state oil company, PERTAMINA, which rapidly grew into a state-within-a-state. It came to an early end, accomplishing the remarkable feat of going bankrupt during the first oil boom. Another state-within-a-state was the Zambian national copper company, ZCCM, which had taken over previously privately owned mines. Its managers gradually and literally ran the operation into the ground, dissipating what had been large profits in the increasing costs of operation. In effect, the value of Zambia's natural assets had been captured by the managers entrusted with them.

Why did Norway and Malaysia succeed where most countries failed? Both had honest leaders, and both had a cadre of public officials with a sense of national purpose. Norway had always been the poor relation within Scandinavia: it had once been a colony of Denmark and long been in the shadow of Sweden. Public officials realized that oil was Norway's chance to catch up. Malaysia was surrounded by hostile countries, and the majority ethnic group, the Bumiputra, was much poorer than the minority Chinese. The public officials who ran the Malaysian national oil company, virtually all from the Bumiputra, realized that it could enable them to catch up. More usually, a sense of national purpose was notably absent: public officials used their positions to benefit nothing larger than their families, and corruption helped them to achieve that objective.

Currently, national-resource companies are very fashionable. I recently attended a meeting in West Africa where half the participants were from oil-rich governments, and the other half from the international oil majors. All that the government officials wanted to talk about was how to establish national oil companies, whereas all that the oil majors wanted to talk about were how their social programs would provide schools and clinics for the local population. I suggested that it might be simpler if they exchanged roles: the governments could become oil companies and the oil companies could become governments. I suspect that much of the impetus for national resource companies is that government budgets are now under greater scrutiny, and the additional opacity provided by sheltering revenues within a government company in which reporting requirements are negligible has become attractive. Without transparency, corruption is almost inevitable: the plunder of natural assets in its crudest form.

The Scale of the Problem

This chapter and the previous one have taken you through the problem of how to raise more money from a country's natural assets: this is the upstream part of harnessing these assets for development. Parts may have seemed obvious and other parts arcane, but cumulatively they have powerful implications. Revenues from natural assets are already by far Africa's most important economic activity. Yet, the way that African governments have sold the extraction rights has generally radically undervalued them. The combination of companies getting deals that have been too generous and their payments being siphoned off by crooked officials has substantially reduced the proportion of the value of natural assets reaching the national treasury. I do not know what that proportion has been over the past few decades, but I would expect it to be closer to 50 percent than to 100 percent.

Yet even these looming problems are dwarfed by those that have beset the discovery process. If Africa really has around as many natural assets per square kilometre as the countries of the OECD, its true asset wealth is around five times what it has found to date. In combination, these problems may have reduced the revenues flowing into African treasuries from the exploitation of nonrenewable natural assets to only around a tenth of their true potential. The scale of problem relegates the debate about whether development aid is too small or too large to a sideshow, yet for every word written about the problems covered in these two chapters, there must have been hundreds, if not thousands of words written about aid.

CHAPTER 6

Selling the Family Silver

HAVING WADED THROUGH THE "UPSTREAM ISSUES"—getting revenue into a country's treasury—it is now time for the "downstream issues"—using the money. This chapter is about a key choice: whether money generated from depleting natural assets should benefit the present or the future. To benefit the present the money should be spent on consumption. To benefit the future it should be saved: consumption should be deferred and revenue from assets used instead to acquire other assets which preserve their value. Economics is a crudely reductionist science and characterizes this choice as very stark. In reality most people get some pleasure from saving, you do not need to have the perverted values of a miser to take some pleasure now in the prospect of being able to consume something in the future. But economists usually abstract from such pleasure: the only thing that gives me happiness now—utility—is current consumption. So saving for the future is a transfer of happiness from now to later. Crude as this is, it surely captures a powerful feature of reality: most of us are not misers, we save because we are prudent. But consuming is more fun.

We have now reached the heart of what is distinctive about the role of government in societies that are rich in nonrenewable natural assets. The exploitation of the natural asset is intrinsically unsustainable. At some stage the oil well is going to run dry, the vein of copper ore will be exhausted, and the revenue stream will cease.

That word "unsustainable" sends shivers down the spine of every environmentalist. But just because the exploitation of a natural asset is unsustainable does not mean that it should be avoided. The only sustainable rate of use of a nonrenewable natural asset is zero. But were we never to use any nonrenewable assets they might as well not be there in the first place: the baby has disappeared with the bathwater. So, literal sustainability sets the bar absurdly high. Here economics is helpful in imagining a more meaningful conception: sustainability does not imply preservation. The world has sustained overall economic growth, albeit with hiccups, for two centuries yet virtually no single economic activity has been sustained. Growth has not been a matter of everything getting bigger. Rather, it has been like running across ice flows: if you stand still you fall in and drown; if you keep going—even if each individual step is unsustainable—you survive. In the nineteenth century the British government was worried that it was going to run out of tall trees for the masts of ships. What happened, of course, is that at a certain point ships no longer needed trees.

The decision to deplete a nonrenewable natural asset is therefore not intrinsically an economic sin. The ethics of depletion depend upon how the money generated gets used. I have suggested that it is ethically incumbent on us to respect the rights of future generations. We may not be the curators of natural assets, but we are the custodians of their value. We are not obliged to turn the earth into a gigantic museum, with nature neatly preserved in its display case. Nonetheless, we have a responsibility not to plunder natural resources because we do not own them in the way that we own created assets. We can fulfill our ethical obligations by bequeathing to the future other kinds of assets of an equivalent value. This boils down to whether to consume the revenues or save them. We have a responsibility to save.

This represents the golden rule for the ethical use of revenue from nonrenewable natural assets. It implies that the use of this revenue should be quite unlike that of normal tax revenue. Normally, tax revenue can be presumed to rise as the economy grows: it is sustainable and thus can be spent on consumption. A good test of whether the government of a resource-rich country is being ethically responsible is whether it has a higher savings rate of its revenues from natural-asset depletion than from other tax revenues. As it depletes the natural asset is it accumulating man-made assets in its place?

Do you have a higher savings rate of unsustainable income than income you expect to continue? Perhaps you have not consciously thought about it; you just have an overall savings rate out of your total income. It might equally be difficult for a government to identify which part of its overall savings is attached to which part of its income. However, we might reasonably expect that those governments whose revenues are largely generated by the depletion of natural assets should have higher savings rates than those whose revenues are fully sustainable. For example, Africa, where so much revenue comes from resource extraction, should tend to have a higher savings rate than "Developing Asia," where revenues are linked to industry. In fact, the opposite is the case. Africa's savings rate averages around 20 percent of national income, whereas that of Developing Asia has been approximately double.

Illusory Revenues

In order to have a high rate of saving from the revenues generated by the depletion of natural assets you need to know what those revenues are. The Publish What You Pay campaign that I introduced in the previous chapter was inspired by the realization that in many resource-rich societies ordinary citizens did not know what those revenues were. Companies and governments were keeping them in the dark about the money that governments received. But the reality is even more problematic: often governments themselves do not realize how much of their revenues accrue from the depletion of natural assets.

Such is the case not because governments are stupid, but because the economy in which they operate sometimes works in mysterious ways. Revenues that appear to be from one source turn out to be from another. Raising tax revenues in many low-income countries is difficult. Much of the economy is "informal," generated by small farmers and street traders. Such people do not keep written accounts; indeed they are often illiterate. Many transactions are for cash and so do not leave a paper trail into which tax collectors can get their teeth. There are too few large formal enterprises for a normal tax base. The one transaction that is easy to tax is imports, which arrive either at a dock or along the road from the coast and so can easily be monitored. What is more, imports always generate a paper trail: they have to be financed and insured. In low-income countries, therefore, the main source of tax revenue is duties on imports.

In a low-income, resource-rich country the two revenues sources—import duties and asset revenue—sit side-by-side on the government budget. Does this imply that the taxes and royalties on the extraction of natural assets are unsustainable, while the duties collected on imports are sustainable? It is not that simple: the underlying source of those import duties depends on what is financing the imports. Imports are financed by exports, and in a resource-rich economy the main exports are extracted natural assets. Often they are the only exports, as for example, in Nigeria, where oil accounts for 98 percent of exports. In the end, exports can only be used to purchase imports, so the tax on imports reduces the value of the exports, dollar-for-dollar. But given that the Nigerian government is the beneficial owner of the oil exports, it is in fact paying its own import duties. So in Nigeria, and other countries that depend upon natural resources for their exports, the independence of the revenue from import duties is a complete illusion. Import duties are merely an indirect way of capturing the oil rents, and a pretty cumbersome and inefficient one to boot.

The upshot is that most governments in low-income, resource-rich countries do not even realize that the overwhelming majority of their revenues stem, directly or indirectly, from the depletion of natural assets and thus are unsustainable. If savings from these revenues is only 20 percent, as in Africa to date, the accumulation of substitute assets will be utterly inadequate to compensate for the exhaustion of the natural assets; revenues will collapse. African societies have failed a key test of good stewardship of natural assets: saving the rents captured by exploitation. If governments do not, we are back in the world of plunder. The plunder I defined in the previous chapter was crude: the value inherent in the natural asset was hijacked by a foreign company or stolen by a corrupt official. In this chapter plunder takes a more subtle form: spending the revenues from depleting resources on consumption. Today's citizens have the power of decision, but if the revenues are used only for consumption the rights of those future citizens are being robbed just as surely as with those cruder forms of plunder.

While getting the revenues properly categorized into those which are sustainable and those which are unsustainable would be helpful, it is only a preliminary. The real action is in setting up distinct decision procedures for their management. The unsustainable revenues need to be protected from the routine pressures for spending on public consumption by rules backed by checks and balances. Decision takers are human beings and so subject to all the usual frailties. As individuals we devise innumerable little disciplines such as deadlines and diets to keep ourselves from temptation. Governments are no different: for consumption out of unsustainable revenues to be held well below that from sustainable revenues institutionalized discipline is likely to be needed.

Sustaining the Unsustainable

But if a 20 percent savings rate is too little, how much is enough? Should all revenue from extracted natural assets be saved? This was the advice that until very recently was given to the governments of resource-rich countries by the International Monetary Fund. However, the reasons were quite different from the ethical argument I set out in part I. The economists of the International Monetary Fund, like most other economists, are Utilitarian, and so we are back to the ethical code in which the objective is "the greatest happiness of the greatest number," interpreted as maximizing utility summed over all people, those alive today and those to come. The Fund then applied a simple theoretical model invented by Milton Friedman known as "Permanent Income." Permanent Income is the conversion of a temporary windfall into an endlessly sustainable level of expenditure. The Permanent Income from a stock of nonrenewable natural assets is easy to calculate. You simply take their capital value—in effect, the valuations made by the World Bank in their snapshot of subsoil assets—and 'imagine that this entire value is invested in international capital markets. The interest income that this invested wealth would generate is then your Permanent Income, which you can spend in perpetuity. The intrinsically unsustainable revenue stream from depleting natural assets has been converted, conceptually, into an equivalent sustainable revenue stream.

The Permanent Income concept not only tells us what the highest level of sustainable consumption would be, it recommends it be chosen. This was not because Milton Friedman was a proto-environmentalist who regarded sustainability as ethically desirable. It was something he derived from his adherence to Utilitarianism. Setting consumption at the maximum sustainable level assumes that people do not get either richer or poorer over time. Remember that Utilitarian preference for equity: extra dollars yield less and less utility so that equity maximizes the sum of utilities. The same applies for equity between time periods: the "greatest happiness" comes from spending the same amount each year. So, following the greatest happiness principle, Permanent Income tells us how much the current generation can spend from its endowment of natural assets. An intrinsically unsustainable flow of income has been converted into its equivalent sustainable level of spending. Continuous consumption at that level produces the greatest possible happiness: utility is being maximized.

In literal terms the conversion of the unsustainable flow of resource revenues into a sustainable flow of consumption works by supposing that the entire stock of natural assets is instantly dug up and invested in financial assets. This is too hypothetical to be realistic as a guide, but even if the natural assets are not all dug up instantly, they would nevertheless yield a rate of return—so long as the world price of the assets appreciates. Is there any reason to expect that it will?

Are Natural Assets Appreciating?

Economics answers that there is a reason, known as the Hotelling Rule after its discoverer. The Hotelling Rule postulates that the price of nonrenewable natural assets will rise over time at what is called the "world interest rate." So, if the interest rate on risk-free assets such as U.S. Treasury Bills is around 4 percent, the price of natural assets should rise by around 4 percent each year. Part of that is simply due to inflation—typically around 2 percent—so that the true rate of increase in the price of natural assets would likely be around 2 percent a year. Why did Hotelling think that this was likely? His idea, which is simple enough, is an early application of the principle of "rational expectations": the notion that information is sufficiently well used that investors' judgments about future values of assets are not systematically wrong. For example, their guess as to what the price of oil will be in 2050 is as likely to be too high as it is too low. The principle of rational expectations has taken a drubbing during the global economic crisis, but before dismissing it, we should explore what it would imply for the path of natural-asset prices. Hotelling's key insight was that natural assets were just one type of asset: leaving oil in the ground until 2050 was as much a decision as keeping U.S. Treasury Bills in your portfolio until 2050. Suppose people expected that the price of oil in 2050 would be $80 per barrel, ten dollars higher than it is today. That increase of only $10 over 40 years yields a lower return that what could be earned by selling the oil today for $70 and investing it for 40 years in U.S. Treasuries. So, the sensible strategy for anyone owning an oil well would be to pump the oil out now and sell it rather than leave it in the ground. As a result the world price of oil today would drop below $70, and, knowing that there would be less oil around in 2050, the expected future price would rise. This would continue until the difference between the price now and the price expected in 2050 was equal to the return on Treasury Bills. The same thing would happen in reverse if the expected price of oil in 2050 was so high—say $300—that leaving oil in the ground looked a much better bet than holding Treasuries.

Suppose therefore that the current generation decided to be guided by the concepts of Permanent Income and the Hotelling Rule. If it digs up all the natural assets it should invest the resulting revenue, though it is entitled to consume the income on that investment because that is sustainable. If it digs up only some of the natural assets it is still entitled to consume the same amount. But now some of the return on the initial value of the natural assets will accrue in the form of the appreciation of natural capital. The present generation is entitled to spend that appreciation but cannot directly get its hands on it; the money does not flow into the national treasury. Indirectly, however, it can spend it by not investing all of the revenues that are generated by the natural assets we extract.

Nobody is very comfortable with the implication of these basic economic concepts. Consuming out of anticipated capital appreciation is potentially very risky. As a graduate student I recall my professor explaining that risk as follows. A shopkeeper does his annual accounts and finds that he has made a loss. But not to worry, this is more than offset by the appreciation in the value of his stock; reassured, he lives by consuming some of it. The next year it is the same story, so he consumes still more of his stock. Finally, there comes a year where he finds he has only three items of stock left to consume: a nail, a hammer, and a rope.

Stock appreciation offers no solid basis for consumption—it can leave you hanging—and the Hotelling Rule is a shaky foundation on which to build expectations of gradually rising prices of natural assets. During the recent commodity boom, when oil spiked to $147, there were hysterical forecasts that the world would run out of oil. The same forecasts had been made during the first oil boom in the 1980s. Sheik Yamani, then the spokesperson for OPEC, the oil cartel, came out with a brilliant riposte to these concerns: "The Stone Age didn't end because the world ran out of stone." I doubt that the Age of Oil will end because the world runs out of oil. Instead, technology will have moved on. Indeed, that has happened repeatedly. The high-value natural assets of the nineteenth century, for example, were nitrates, which are far less valuable now. The world prices of commodities can be tracked for over a century. From these data there is little basis for concluding that prices are rising; indeed, other than for oil they may even have been falling.

Technological changes alone should not be enough to disprove the Hotelling Rule. If people properly anticipate those changes—which, according to the rational expectations assumption, they will do—then different types of assets should still follow precisely the same course for prices. But the Hotelling Rule does not allow for the costs of extracting natural assets, which are not, in fact, like a Treasury Bill. If I come to think that U.S. Treasuries are not a wise investment then I can sell them all today. But if I come to think that copper will not appreciate at the world interest rate, I cannot suddenly extract it all at once. I can choose to extract the contents of a copper belt more rapidly, but this will be costly because I will need to sink more mines and each one will depreciate over a shorter horizon. I may therefore have to accept a lower expected return on keeping the copper in the ground in order to avoid those extraction costs. But those extra extraction costs are a certainty: I will definitely have to pay them to extract the copper more rapidly. On the other hand, the future course of the world copper price is, frankly, anybody's guess. Simply look at how the prices of the major natural assets have changed. In 1998 oil was $10 a barrel, and by 2008 it was $147 per barrel before dropping to $37 per barrel.

In view of this radical uncertainty, few resource-extraction companies work on the Hotelling Rule. Rather, they tend to think of a technologically-driven, long-term average world price and work around that. Periodically they may revise this price upward, but that is not the same as relying on Hotelling. They do not even work on a likely frequency distribution of world prices because they do not have much confidence that the future distribution will look like the past distribution. Why should it? We know from the past that prices are highly volatile, but the sort of volatility experienced, say, between the First and the Second World Wars was driven by technologies and economies that have been entirely superseded.

One result of this radical uncertainty is that a resource-rich low-income country cannot count on natural assets it has left in the ground becoming more valuable, and therefore a good investment. The really good investments are made above—not below—ground, but they depend upon sound management of the investment process.

A Bird in the Hand

There was therefore good reason for a more cautious approach, one that did not count on the appreciation of natural assets left in the ground. Nonetheless, the Fund, a naturally cautious institution, took these concerns to their logical extreme. It modified the Permanent Income principle by adding one of its own, called the "Bird-in-the-Hand Rule": future revenues from natural assets should not be anticipated; rather, only those revenues that actually came in should be counted. Not only might prices not rise, they might collapse. The costs of extracting known reserves might turn out to be far higher than anticipated, squeezing the rents correspondingly. At the worst, those supposedly known reserves might turn out not to be there after all. This caution translated operationally into a rule whereby all revenue from extraction should be saved. Only the investment income from these savings ought to be spent on consumption. Since the stock of savings builds up gradually, the investment income in the first few years of resource extraction is very small, permitting very little extra consumption. Indeed, in the first year consumption is zero. In the second year, the revenues of the first year have been invested in Treasury Bills at 4 percent, meaning consumption of 4 percent of the first year revenues would be permitted, and so forth. It takes many years of forbearance before a country would be able to consume anything approaching what if it could consume if it opted for plunder.

Unsurprisingly, governments in many of the countries where new discoveries have been made have not been too enthusiastic about taking this advice. On the news of the discovery of an abundant natural asset, citizens look forward to rapid relief from their poverty, and politicians look forward to the prospect of large increases in public spending. Into this joyous mix come the Fund economists in their dark suits and advise that for the next few years virtually all revenue should be saved. This is not what people want to hear. In 2007 Ghana discovered oil. Prior to the discovery Ghana's fiscal policy was prudent: its fiscal deficit was less than 2 percent of GDP. Yet by December 2008, before any oil had actually been extracted, the deficit had exploded to an estimated 19 percent of GDP. When the oil arrives it is expected to generate revenues of between 4 and 5 percent of GDP, so the government hastily spent around four times the revenues that it anticipated.

However, more prudent governments take the advice seriously because it approximates quite closely what the Norwegian government has been doing with its oil revenues. Revenues from natural assets are placed into a special public fund known as the Sovereign Wealth Fund, which is earmarked for future generations and invested in international capital markets. Although stock markets are very volatile, overall the system has served Norway well: according to the 2009 Human Development Index it offers the best quality of life in the world. Unsurprisingly, it has become a model for those governments of low-income countries which wish to behave responsibly. Indeed, I was told that the Norwegian government had received requests for advice from 50 other governments on how to manage their resource revenues. Due to the success of Norway, the Fund's advice has had far greater impact than might otherwise have been the case.

The Fund's Bird-in-the-Hand advice has the virtue of protecting the interest of the future. But is it right for a low-income country? There are two key reasons for thinking it too severe.

The most obvious reason is that it is hyper-cautious. The bottom billion countries should indeed avoid dangerously risky strategies, such as consuming anticipated price appreciation. But their entire society is already threatened by the multiple risks associated with poverty. Doing everything to avoid the highly unlikely worst-possible scenario—that the revenue from resource extraction ceases tomorrow—condemns people to endure hardships that could be remedied by spending. A better approach is to assess the risks and then estimate a reasonable worst case scenario, one that is conservative but does not assume that the world will end tomorrow. This estimated future stream of natural-resource revenue can then be channeled into the Permanent Income equivalent: in other words, spending on consumption can start at a safely sustainable level immediately rather than wait for an investment portfolio to build up.

In principle, a conservative estimate of the future revenue stream might justify some initial borrowing to finance early consumption. Other than in moments of financial crisis—as in the past year—the commercial banks will be queuing up to proffer such loans. But there are powerful reasons to be wary. Commercial loans carry high interest rates and if there are unanticipated delays in the revenue stream a future government might be caught in difficulties, such as late-payment penalties. Perhaps the most persuasive reason against borrowing for early consumption, however, is that this is precisely what a plundering government would choose to do. Citizens need to be able to judge from the actions of their government whether it is a plunderer or a custodian. Only a few actions are readily observable to citizens; one of them is borrowing. A custodial government can signal its good intentions by choosing highly visible strategies. Deciding not to borrow is one such signal.

Nevertheless, early consumption may be warranted. Signature bonuses from extraction companies provide a no-risk way of anticipating revenue in that they do not have to be paid back. But they are still liable to be expensive: they carry an implicit interest rate which may be quite high.

The Need for Capital

Not only is the Bird-in-the-Hand Rule excessively cautious, there is a deeper reason why the Fund's advice was too austere. Low-income countries are short of capital. Behind that statement of the obvious lurks the full awful grimness of poverty: the stench from slums that lack drains; the illiteracy from a lack of schools; the crops that rot because of a lack of roads to market, the lives wasted from a lack of jobs. Yes, low-income countries are chronically short of capital. An implication is that, so long as investment is done reasonably well, the return on additional capital should be high, indeed much higher than the tiny return on U.S. Treasury Bills. That caveat—"so long as investment is done reasonably well"—is fundamental, but for the moment put it aside.

How big might the return be on investment in a low-income country, conditional upon it being done reasonably well? Michael Spence, a Nobel Laureate in economics, gave me the key insight here: the overall return is likely to be big because the benefits of the investment are diffused right across the economy. A new road might enable a new crop to be grown and exported; the income from those exports might increase the demand for bicycles, inducing entry of new retailers and so making the market more competitive; the lower price of bicycles might enable more families to keep children in school. In other words, the return works through such a myriad of channels that it cannot be captured by the simple techniques of cost-benefit analysis. Even if not as measurable, it is likely to be considerably higher than the return on U.S. Treasury Bills.

How does this affect how much can ethically be consumed immediately from the revenue generated by resource extraction? Recently, Tony Venables worked out the answer using the same economic Utilitarianism used by the Fund itself. As he showed, if the return on investment is high when capital is scarce the economy should be able to enjoy a phase of rapid growth while it catches up with the rest of the world. The future citizens of the country will therefore be much richer than the impoverished citizens of today. At this point the Utilitarian calculus of equity kicks in: those future citizens should count for less, not because they are in the future but because they are rich. Consumption needs to be brought forward to the present in order to redistribute income in such a way as to maximize total utility—the greatest happiness of the greatest number. This does not licence consuming all the money now, but it implies that a moderate proportion of the revenues should be consumed now rather than saved. The Fund was sufficiently interested in this to publish our work in its journal.

You may have spotted a contradiction in my thinking—even an apparent schizophrenia: between supporting an analysis that depends upon the Utilitarian framework and simultaneously critiquing that framework. The schizophrenia was temporary: I no longer accept the Utilitarian perspective of our obligations to the future. Just because future citizens will be richer than today's citizens does not give us the right to their assets. Poverty does not justify plunder.

What happens when we switch from the ethics of economic Utilitarianism to the ethics of custody? The ethics of custody does not require a low-income country to adopt the Bird-in-the-Hand Rule. If domestic investment has a high return we can more easily meet our obligations to the future. Suppose that the return on U.S. Treasury Bills remains around 4 percent while the return on domestic investment is around 8 percent. The difference between these two rates of return gives us wiggle room in which to meet our obligations. The custody principle dictates that we should not infringe the rights of the future; if we use up a natural asset we must hand on to the future other assets of equivalent value. But if we extract $1 million worth of natural assets and invest the money domestically in something that generates $80,000 per year, we have an asset which at prevailing world interest rates will be valued at $2 million. The unusually favorable investment opportunities in our economy imply that by switching our composition of assets from natural assets to domestic investment we can make a capital gain. However, we do not need to bequeath $2 million of substitute assets to the future: after all, we have only depleted natural assets valued at $1 million. As long as we can genuinely earn 8 percent on our domestic investment, we can fully compensate the future for that depletion by saving and investing only half, or $500,000. Since that will generate $40,000 per year the capital gain on the investment raises its market value to $1 million.

Of course, it is not good enough just to assume that the return on investment will be twice as high as the world interest rate. Were such the case, why wouldn't private investors made these investments? The answer is that private investors face political risks that public investment does not, and the high return may be dependent upon actions that the government has not yet taken but are within its power. While, of course, the numbers I have used are merely illustrative, they do suggest a workable justification for the immediate consumption of natural assets by a low-income country. A prudent government does not need to imitate Norway, saving 100 percent of the revenues, then investing them on the world financial market and hence getting a return of around 4 percent. Such a strategy makes sense for Norway because it already has an enormous amount of capital invested in Norway. Indeed, as of the millennium, Norway had more man-made capital per head of the population than any other country on earth. It has wonderful public capital such as transport infrastructure and schools, and abundant private capital such as oil rigs and ships. A fair guess is that the rate of return on yet more capital invested in Norway would be quite modest. It therefore makes sense to spread the investment that matches Norway's depletion of its natural assets around the world. It also makes sense for Norway to have a savings rate of around 100 percent. In fact, in the case of Norway it makes no difference whether you apply Utilitarianism or the ethics of custody: in either case the necessary savings rate would come out to be around 100 percent.

Under what circumstances would it be right for the government of a resource-rich, low-income country to choose to imitate Norway's investment strategy? The choice would be reasonable if the government believed that it would not realistically be able to invest productively in its own country's economy. For example, public investments have to be implemented by public officials and if the civil service is corrupt such investments would be lost. Should the government take the bleak view that nothing can be done about this the custody framework drives us straight back to the 100 percent savings rate.

Where does this leave matters? Revenues from natural assets are distinctive: they are not like other tax revenues because they are unsustainable. If the present generation extracts natural assets custody requires that future generations be properly compensated; if they are not they have been plundered. The Norwegian model calls for all resource-derived revenues to be saved and invested in world financial markets. But for a low-income country, following that model means that today's urgent needs go unmet while money piles up in New York banks. It is only sensible if the government takes a despairingly bleak view of domestic investment. If it can invest well domestically, then a much more attractive option opens up. The interests of the future can be fully protected while a substantial proportion of the revenues can be used for consumption. Quite what that proportion is depends upon the rate of return on domestic assets relative to that on leaving the natural asset in the ground. But even on generous assumptions, the investment rate out of the revenues from natural assets should be considerably higher than that from other revenues. In Africa the overall investment rate as a proportion of income has been lower than in any other region: it has averaged less than 20 percent.

Boom Time

I have argued that the government of a resource-rich low-income country has an ethical responsibility to future citizens, requiring it to invest a substantial proportion of the revenues it receives from sales of natural assets. It makes sense gradually to sell the family silver: there are better investments than silver. That is the responsible way of handling the depletion which is intrinsic to the exploitation of nonrenewable assets.

However, depletion is a slow burn, and might take several decades. Sometimes there is a far more compelling argument for refraining from the consumption of revenues from natural assets: boom time.

The world prices of commodities are volatile. They are, in fact, wildly volatile. Analysts use the history of past prices to estimate the range within which the price next year is likely to lie. The range conventionally estimated is that which has a 95 percent chance of being right. As of January 2008 the range for the oil price in January 2009 was $65 to $210. Two things about this statistical forecast are equally striking. One was that the range, for a mere twelve months ahead, was so wide as to be virtually useless. The other was that the actual price, $37, was well outside (on the lower end) even that wide range. Nor is this wholly exceptional; prices have always been volatile. However, the booms and the busts tend not to be symmetrical: the path of prices does not look like a wavy line, with curvy bumps matched by curvy troughs. Rather, the pattern tends to be one of sharp spikes followed by long periods of decline (the commodity boom of 2005–8 currently looks to have fit this pattern). There are simple reasons for this pattern. When prices fall it is possible either to stockpile output, or simply to shut down production. In principle, the flow of supply onto the market can drop to zero and this response cushions the price decline. But when prices rise there is a physical limit to how much stocks can be drawn down, and to how rapidly output can be expanded. As these limits are reached, the only way of maintaining a balance between supply and demand is to choke off the rising demand with yet higher prices. Hence the spikes.

This pattern of boom and bust has profound implications for the management of the revenues from natural resources. During a boom, such as the one that ended in 2008, most of the revenues are doubly unsustainable. Not only are the high revenues derived from the sale of a depleting asset, they cannot be relied upon to be sustained for more than a few years. How many years is anybody's guess; commodity prices cannot be forecast. Even as late as the summer of 2008 many were expecting the high prices to persist, perhaps for decades, as Asia's meteoric economic growth created a voracious demand for natural resources. The unexpected price crash was salutary: it reminded governments that resource revenues are precarious.

Booms do not arrive neatly labeled "temporary." The best predictions as to their duration use a long-term moving average of prices as a guide. When the current price is above this benchmark the excess revenues should be regarded as unlikely to persist for long. If these excess revenues are used to increase consumption, in a few years time they are likely to be cut back down again. There lies the mixed blessing of living for the moment: increasing consumption creates joy, cutting consumption induces pain. Psychological evidence suggests that the pain of the cuts exceeds the joy of the highs. Economists believe this to be due to habit-formation: once people get used to a level of consumption it is agonizing suddenly not to be able to satisfy those habits. One of the benefits of rising prosperity in the rich countries is that in recent decades fewer people have had to experience this agony, but pick up any nineteenth-century novel and you are likely to find a fallen member of the gentry. Fear of impoverishment haunts many of these novels.

If consumption cannot be cut during busts, it should also not be increased during booms. An apparent solution would be to shift the volatility in revenue from the government to the resource-extraction companies. In principle this can be done by design of the tax system: the companies make huge profits when prices are high, offset by losses when prices are low. But this is a dangerous strategy. The extractive industries tend to base their investment on the long-term average world price of a commodity. Being offered a sweetener in the form of low taxation when prices are unusually high is welcome, but it is unlikely that the companies will feel sufficiently confident about the chances of high prices to warrant paying much for the privilege. Further, the company may, quite reasonably, discount any promise of low taxes at times of high prices due to the time-consistency problem.

But if revenues are highly volatile and consumption cannot be adjusted something still must give. The only thing left is savings. They should be very high during the booms so that they can be much lower during the troughs. And if savings are invested domestically in order to reap higher returns than those available on world capital markets, that investment, too, is going to be volatile. There are limits as to how volatile investment can be without the quality of that investment deteriorating, so it is sensible to cushion the changes in investment by placing much of the peak revenues on world capital markets. Thus, in boom time we are at least part-way back to the Norwegian model: save some of the money in world financial markets rather than spend it domestically. The rationale, however, is different. The financial assets we acquire are not to be kept in perpetuity for future generations, but only until such time as they can efficiently be used to finance domestic investment. This should in turn influence the sort of financial assets we acquire. Because the Norwegian model envisages that investments are held for a very long time, fluctuations in the underlying prices of the assets acquired are not very important. What matters is the long-term average rate of return. In contrast, if we are going to need to bring the money back to the country within a few years to finance domestic investment—build schools and hospitals—we should be rather more careful to protect its short-term value. We should therefore invest more cautiously when placing money abroad. Such caution comes at a price. The return on assets that are safe and liquid, such as U.S. Treasury Bills, will be modest. That in turn implies that we will need to save a yet higher proportion of the revenues during boom time. To compensate for $1 million-worth of extracted natural assets we will no longer be able to get away with saving only $500,000 and relying on a high return to magnify those savings into a man-made asset worth $1 million. We will need to save something closer to $1 million.

The big picture is that a resource-dependent economy is unavoidably volatile, swinging between booms and busts. Inflicting that volatility on consumption would be too painful. So the volatility must be offset by savings: boom times will basically mean only boom savings, not a consumption party. Because the economy is short of capital it makes sense for the government to deploy those savings in its own economy rather than on international financial markets. But there are limits to how volatile that domestic investment can be without making the country unstable. So during boom time much of the savings will need to be parked abroad temporarily in safe, liquid financial assets. The role of those savings abroad is to smooth the investment process. Rather than a Sovereign *Wealth* Fund the country needs a Sovereign *Liquidity* Fund of short-term assets to buffer the shocks to revenue.

How far should such buffering go?

Simulations based on the past volatility of commodity prices suggest that in order fully to smooth out the highs and the lows, and spending versus saving, a very large Liquidity Fund would be needed. To build such a fund would take all the revenues for many years. The cost of such a strategy in terms of postponed domestic investment would defeat the purpose: virtually all the savings would go into low-yielding foreign financial assets instead of into the domestic economy. While some smoothing is essential, resource-rich economies that want to invest domestically will need to learn how to live with investment volatility.

Plundering the Future

The central point of this chapter has been to determine an ethically responsible choice for a low-income society between depleting revenue generated by extraction of natural assets for consumption and depleting them for savings. An ethically responsible choice respects reasonable obligations to the future. It requires the present generation to save a substantial proportion of the revenue. What "substantial" means depends, both on the return on domestic investment, and upon where world prices are relative to their long-term average.

Politically, foregoing consumption in favor of the future is not easy. In 2003 a group of economic reformers was appointed to senior political positions in Nigeria. They immediately recognized that the oil revenues were being plundered, not just in the sense of the crudest form—outright theft—although there was plenty of that, but in a more sophisticated manner: the savings rate out of the depleting oil revenues was negligible. Further, as the oil boom intensified before their eyes, the reformers realized that because prices were likely to be unsustainably high, savings were needed to cushion a future drop. They explained this to the Nigerian Senate using the homely analogy of the need to save for a rainy day. The response from Senators was "It's raining now!" Of course, part of their opposition to a high savings rate was because they would benefit in proportion to the spending that they authorized, not the saving. Nonetheless, this illustrates how difficult is the political struggle involved with saving natural-resource revenues.

How successful, on average, has that struggle been? To answer, we should distinguish between the long-term rationale, depletion, and the boom-time rationale. Until recently there has been no overall guide as to whether the long-term depletion of natural assets is being matched by the accumulation of other assets. In principle, national income accounts, which purport to show what in total a country earned and spent each year, should have provided an answer. However, although national income accounting has been around for over sixty years, it was designed for the rich countries of the world where natural assets are only a minor part of the economy, so such issues were ignored. The result was that when the technique came to be applied to low-income, resource-rich countries, their income was exaggerated. Think why: nearly half of Nigeria's national income, as reported by conventional national accounting, comes from the extraction of oil. But what Nigeria is actually doing here is not generating income, so much as selling an asset. If you sell your house you do not treat the revenue from the sale as if it were just another part of this year's income. But that is precisely what the Nigerian national accounts are doing. There is a way of correcting national accounts for this error. It is known as "Green Accounting." In essence, the depletion of natural assets is subtracted from apparent income unless offset by the accumulation of other assets. To date, the most convincing attempt at Green Accounting for the countries of the bottom billion has been done by a team led by Nobel laureate Kenneth Arrow. They have built a more comprehensive measure of wealth for the period 1970–2000, one that included natural assets alongside all the man-made assets. I rely on their estimates, as recently adapted by Professor Sir Partha Dasgupta, a distinguished Indian economist at Cambridge University.

What happens when Africa's national accounts are redone on this basis? Results reveal that over these three decades, comprehensive wealth per person declined by 2.8 percent per year. By the end of these thirty years comprehensive wealth had more than halved: the family silver was rapidly being sold to finance consumption. Ordinary citizens would not have recognized this plunder from their own experience; living standards were barely being maintained. But even this was being achieved only by voraciously eating into natural capital. So the evidence points to plunder on a massive scale during this period: the present generation was depleting the future of its natural assets without providing compensation.

The recent commodity booms set a different challenge, and the question is whether they were recognized as temporary bonanzas which required a high savings rate, or spent on consumption. The evidence here is more mixed. For at least the period between 2003 and 2007 the Nigerian economic reform team read the boom for what it was and slammed up the savings rate. By the end of the boom Nigeria had accumulated an impressive $70 billion in foreign assets, an amount larger than the British foreign exchange reserves. The reformers had all lived through the squandered boom of 1973–86 and were determined that history would not be repeated. Ordinary Nigerians owe them a massive debt of gratitude.

Did other countries learn from the mistakes of the past? Among Africa's other oil exporters, the two North African countries— Algeria and Libya—do seem to have sharply increased their savings during the boom. But, at least judging from the data I have seen, no signs of prudence emerged from the other major African oil economies—Chad, Cameroon, Angola, Gabon, and the Sudan. Taking Africa as a whole, on the eve of the boom in 2003, the rate of savings was modest: around a fifth of national income. During the boom years of 2004–8 savings did increase, but only by around 4 percentage points. And what was done with these savings? Since these economies are chronically short of capital, there should have been any number of opportunities for domestic investment that offered higher returns than saving on the world capital market. That being the case, saving the money abroad would be tantamount to despair: an admission that the implementation of investment is drastically deficient. Yet, sadly, even the modest increase in savings was substantially invested abroad: the increase in domestic investment during the boom was on average less than 2 percent. For comparison, Asia, which is not resource-rich and so does not need to offset significant depletion of natural assets, had an average domestic investment rate of 37 percent during the years of the commodity boom. Its savings rate was even higher: as a result China amassed two trillion dollars worth of U.S. Treasuries. Africa's investment rate during the boom was a mere 23 percent.

Chinese Deals as a Commitment Technology

One reason it has proved so politically difficult to meet the reasonable ethical obligations of the future is that the hard work of a prudent government may be undone by a future imprudent one. During the oil boom the Nigerian reformers prudently built up $70 billion in liquid foreign financial assets, but will that savings get converted into domestic investment or will it instead be used for consumption? If it ends up being used for consumption, all the reformers will have achieved is a transfer of the political capital that comes of throwing a consumption party from their own vintage of politicians to their successors.

Ideally, what a prudent government needs is a means of locking in the decision to save so that it cannot be reversed. The Nigerian reformers recognized this and chose a legislative approach. They proposed a Fiscal Responsibility Bill, empowering the Finance Minister to determine a prudent saving rate. Nigeria is a federation and half of the oil revenues accrue to the thirty-six states rather than to the federal government. Therefore in addition to the federal bill, an equivalent one was needed for each state. The federal bill was enacted during the boom, but even by the time the boom ended only seven of the states had enacted equivalent legislation. Might there be an alternative way for a prudent finance minister to lock the society into irreversible saving?

Inadvertently, China has been providing one. For the past decade China has been busy doing deals in Africa, purchasing the rights to resource extraction in exchange for the construction of infrastructure. Recall that the international agencies hated these deals. Resource-extraction rights were not being sold for revenues that could flow into the national treasury, and then used by the government to build the same infrastructure. Instead, there was a complete budgetary bypass. As a result, the deals were utterly opaque; they could not be subjected to proper scrutiny.

Clearly, that lack of scrutiny would have been one attraction: a corrupt politician might prefer to sell the rights to the nation's natural assets under a veil of secrecy. But from my talks with politicians, I began to see why a Chinese-style deal might also be attractive to the reformers. Any prudent Minister of Finance could see that an investment rate of just 23 percent was too little. Yet he might justifiably be afraid of being but one voice in favor of spending much of the money on infrastructure. Across the table, the Minister of Defense might argue that now was the time to raise army salaries. He might mention that there had been disaffection in the ranks and then look meaningfully at the President. The Minister of Education would interject that the teachers unions were fully aware that extra money had flowed into the budget and were planning a strike. In short, the Minister of Finance might reasonably fear that the bulk of the money—77 percent—would dribble away in extra recurrent spending. Compared with that outcome, the Chinese deal might look rather attractive. There would be no extra money to carve up at the cabinet table: the offer was for infrastructure. The investment rate out of the implicit revenues would therefore be 100 percent. By accepting the deal the minister locked in the investment decision: it became time-consistent. If the Chinese deals were as one-sided as the international agencies suspected, the Minister was caught between Scylla and Charybdis: plunder of the country's future by its present generation, or plunder of the country's present by the Chinese.

Suppose the minister wanted to keep that commitment mechanism—locking in investment by bypassing the budget—but also wanted to ensure that the Chinese deal was fair. There is, in fact, a straightforward way to go about it. What was missing in those Chinese deals was competition. The Chinese were the only ones offering rights to natural resources in return for infrastructure. Other potential extractors had simply not yet realized that the Chinese had hit on a promising new approach. Instead of entering into a secret deal with the Chinese, the government could have publicly auctioned the rights for resource extraction—but for infrastructure instead of for money. The Chinese government had put together a consortium of a resource-extraction company, a construction company, and some aid, as part of their offer. Others could do the same and an auction take place. The auction would specify the extraction rights, as in a normal auction, but the bidding would have been in terms of how far down a specified list of desired infrastructure the consortium was willing to go instead of how much money it would pay. Were the Chinese to win such auctions it would be because they had made the best-value offers. Instead of accusing the Chinese of plundering Africa, it might have been more effective of the international community to imitate them.

Unmet Obligations

"Plunder" is an emotionally charged word, one which conjures up images of piracy and violence. But plunder is, at its root, an economic concept—the abrogation of property rights—and it can take more subtle forms than theft. To date, in the low-income countries natural assets have been plundered by the present generation: insufficient regard has been paid to the reasonable rights of future generations. Such plunder has occurred both through the slow burn of depletion and the quick high of bonanza. That deprived future generation is not just the hypothetical: most Africans alive today are too young to vote. In the last chapter I argued that part of the value of natural assets had been plundered in the crudest sense both by foreign companies and by small domestic elites. This chapter has shown that problem is compounded by a more subtle form of plunder. Today's adults are a minority that has abused its power. Recently, I discussed these ideas with a minister from the Cameroons. When I came to the need to separate out the unsustainable revenues, he asked what if virtually all revenue was oil-derived and hence unsustainable. He could, of course, see the implication: savings would need to be high. And he could see that in the Cameroons it was already too late. Past government decisions have

effectively locked the society into public consumption. But for
other societies it is not too late. In September 2009, along the coast
from the Cameroons, Sierra Leone discovered oil. Decisions over
the next few years will determine whether the current generation
saves or plunders the oil revenues.

The decision to save revenues is important, but is by itself not
enough. The counsel of despair must be overcome, and the resource-
rich countries of the bottom billion must successfully invest in their
own societies.

CHAPTER 7

Investing in Investing

HARNESSING NATURAL ASSETS for sustained development depends upon a chain of decisions, and the outcome is only as good as the weakest link in that chain. We have now reached the last link in the chain, and unfortunately it is the weakest.

Suppose that the government has got each of the three previous decisions right: It has commissioned geological surveys that have revealed sufficient information about opportunities and thus been able to auction extraction rights for likely discoveries at good prices; it has designed a tax system which has captured the lion's share of the rents that constitute the economic value of these natural assets; and it has saved the bulk of these revenues—less than 100 percent—because it judged some extra consumption to be consistent with meeting its obligations to the future, and, recognizing that the rate of return on domestic investment would be much higher than the world interest rate, counted on a capital gain to ease the burden of responsibility. All that remains—the final link—is to implement that domestic investment.

Scaling up domestic investment is surely the very stuff of development: it builds the office blocks, constructs the factories, paves the roads, and generates the electricity that visibly distinguishes an emerging market economy from the bottom billion. Why might this final step be the most difficult?

Recall that the International Monetary Fund has advised the governments of low-income countries to use the savings from the revenues on natural resources not to invest domestically but to acquire foreign financial assets. This is the Norwegian model, to which the more prudent finance ministers of poorer countries have been attracted. The Fund's advice is based on a realistic sense of the problems involved: were the extra money spent on domestic investment it would be unlikely to yield an adequate return. Indeed, it might actually damage the economy by congesting fragile public investment systems and causing a collapse in quality. The overarching concept the Fund uses for these problems is "absorption": the economy simply cannot absorb the extra spending. Indeed, the Fund has the same concern about aid, except that the revenues from natural resources are potentially even more problematic. They are concentrated into brief periods of boom, and, unlike aid, do not come with an army of aid workers helping to implement projects.

Here is an example of why the Fund is skeptical about domestic investment. In April 2009 the Nigerian government announced that it would spend $5 billion of the savings accumulated during the recently deceased oil boom on investing in electricity generation. The announcement attracted attention because improvements in electricity supply were so manifestly needed; a lack of power has been the single greatest constraint on economic activity. But before celebrating the change, we should reflect a moment on why Nigeria is so chronically short of electricity. The answer is not because of a lack of investment. It is because the money was siphoned off. In fact,

in a *Wall Street Journal* article on April 28, 2009, the government estimated that around $16 billion of previous investment expenditure
on the sector has been misappropriated. The critical issue for the
Nigerian government is whether the $5 billion will be better spent.

For $16 billion of government spending on electricity generation
to have been misappropriated many public officials and politicians
must have made an awful lot of money. Given that since 1998 Nigeria
has been a democracy, why was there so little effective scrutiny?

By chance a Nigerian named Nuhu Ribadu came as a visitor to
my research center at Oxford. Nuhu Ribadu is a policeman, and
while at Oxford is writing up his reflections about his job. I hope
he will tell the world not just what happened but in the way that
he told it to me: in gentle understatements that belie, but cannot
disguise, their dramatic content. Nuhu's authority in Nigeria was
quite considerable and originated from the fall-out of 9/11. The
American government was quite reasonably concerned to close off
international financial flows to terrorists and, together with a group
of developed countries, established a task force—the Financial
Action Task Force—to address the problem. The Task Force drew
up a list of countries that it deemed did not have sufficient scrutiny
of their financial systems to ensure that they were not conduits for
terrorist money. Nigeria was placed on that list.

To his credit, President Obasanjo of Nigeria recognized that this
represented a potential threat to Nigeria's reputation, which was
the overarching mission of his presidency. He had been a founding leader of Transparency International and wanted to confront
the corruption that pervaded his country. By 2002 he had secured
the legislation that established a new investigative authority, the
Economic and Financial Crimes Commission, and had appointed
Nuhu to be in charge of it. He told Nuhu to do whatever it took to
get Nigeria off that list. Nuhu did just that.

Like others, I have been a strong advocate of international standards and codes. This story demonstrates both their potential power and how negligent we have been in using them. The Financial Action Task Force was not meant to help the fight against corruption in Nigeria; it was organized exclusively for our own interest in reducing the risk of terrorist attacks. Yet arguably it did more to improve conditions in Nigeria than all the other efforts of the international community since Nigerian independence.

Nuhu led a team of forty police officers: forty officers facing a sea of corruption. His strategy was to start at the top. If corruption was to be countered, it was no good chasing the lowly officials among whom corruption was a survival strategy. It was essential to go after high-profile officials, whose prosecution would send shock waves through the Nigerian elite. Nuhu did not balk at the political risks. Among many others he arrested the President of the Nigerian Senate. He also successfully prosecuted his own boss, the Inspector General of Police.

Nuhu had noticed, and indeed how could anyone not have noticed, that in all those years of grand corruption, whether because of incompetence or design, there had not been a single successful prosecution. He discovered that his boss had, in total, amassed savings of $150 million. This was the counterpart to that $16 billion and the other money plundered by public officials in the course of their jobs as controllers of public spending programs. Avoiding scrutiny had been expensive: $150 million had ended up with this one person, so presumably much more had been needed to appease others charged with the task of scrutiny. Such huge bribes permitted plunder counted not in millions but in billions. Nuhu came to Oxford because after the end of the final term of President Obasanjo he prosecuted one big fish too many. Indeed, at the time of his arrival he was himself facing prosecution. I was harboring a man wanted for the crime of not wearing a uniform.

Nigeria is not alone in finding corruption to be a major impediment to implementing an effective public-investment program. There is a simple reason why such investments are more prone to corruption that other forms of spending. Capital, which is what investment buys, comes in two forms: equipment and structures (think trucks and roads). Public investment predominantly takes the form of structures; private investment predominantly equipment. The countries of the bottom billion do not produce their own equipment, and since they buy it on the world market it is reasonably easy to tell whether the price they paid is excessive. Structures, on the other hand, have to be produced domestically by the construction sector, and globally the construction sector is second only to the resource-extraction sector itself in its reputation for corruption. Each construction project is subtly different: it has to fit on a particular site, relying on skills and inputs such as cement that may be in short supply. Quite often the details of design change during construction, so modifications need to be negotiated. All these idiosyncratic features make it difficult to tell whether the price of any particular construction deal has been inflated by corruption. Even competitive tendering is relatively easy to counter. For example, a corrupt company might reach an agreement with the official in charge of awarding the contract. The company wins the contract with the lowest bid, but then, as the work progresses, the official changes the specification and the modifications, which cannot be subjected to competitive bidding, turn out to be remarkably costly. So, a large public investment program is dependent upon a sector which is globally corrupt.

Yet the problems of absorbing a large investment program cannot be universal. Asia, for example, is investing a far higher proportion of its income than is Africa. Suppose that the resource-rich countries of the bottom billion were to increase their investment rate from around 20 percent to around 30 percent—still well below developing Asia, but nevertheless a quantum change. Why, apart from corruption, might this make things go wrong?

Are There Investment Opportunities?

Could the reason why investment in Africa is so modest simply be because it does not offer a high return? After all, investors vote with their wallets. Jean-Louis Warnholz, one of my students, determined to investigate whether this was the case. He triangulated three distinct sources on the rate of return on private investment. One was the return on direct American investment, region-by-region. A second was the return on equity invested in stock markets around the world. The third assembled survey evidence from 18,000 manufacturing firms drawn from over thirty countries. Just getting all this information was a major undertaking, and it then had to be made as comparable as possible. But what Jean-Louis found made the effort worthwhile. By all three measures the rate of return on private investment in Africa was higher than in any other region. The *Harvard Business Review* regarded these results as so astonishing that in 2009 it featured them in its annual roundup of "the 20 breakthrough ideas of the year." The following month *Newsweek* magazine promoted us to one of "the top ten world ideas of 2009." Perhaps by the time you are reading this it will have been declared the "idea of the decade," but the pertinent point is that a low return on capital is unlikely to be the explanation for Africa's investment problem.

However, it is one thing to have a high average return, quite another to have a high return at the margin—meaning the return on additional investment. Yet the return at the margin and beyond is what matters for inducing a large increase in investment. Were investment substantially increased without changes in practices, the presumption should be that the rate of return on this additional investment would be lower than on existing investment, quite possibly much lower. Unless "project selection"—the choice of investment opportunities—is truly awful, those projects already being chosen have a higher return than those lower down the list. The first few obvious investments indeed have an amazing return, but they are a misleading guide as to whether there are many equivalent opportunities. Not only would extra projects come from further down the list, but the capacity to implement them would be spread more thinly. The investment program might become congested and inefficient.

The "absorption" problem of managing increased investment is real enough. Nonetheless, the Fund's past conclusion that the solution is to save abroad rather than invest domestically is costly defeatism. Few low-income societies can realistically aspire to be *rentier* states, such as Kuwait, with citizens living off the income generated by financial assets held in New York. These societies are mostly only resource-rich in the sense of having plentiful natural assets relative to their man-made assets. A few tiny societies, such as Equatorial Guinea, could potentially become like Kuwait, but all the major societies will ultimately need to develop their domestic economies to reach even middle-income levels. They cannot continue to duck the challenge of investing a much higher proportion of their income within the economy, and doing so productively. That, ultimately, is the core task facing all of the major low-income, resource-rich societies. Everything up to this point has merely been a prelude.

The task can be split into three quite distinct components, each of which would need to happen in order for a society to experience a quantum leap in the rate of investment without crashing the rate of return upon it. First and foremost, the government would need to improve its management of public investment. But that is not enough. Part of the return on public investment depends on it inducing complementary private investment, which depends upon decisions over which the government has no control. Still, while the government cannot dictate private investment, it can make it more attractive by improving the policy environment.

Suppose that both public and private investment increase substantially. Is that enough? Probably not, because in the economies of the bottom billion public and private investment share a common obstacle: capital goods are already expensive and when investment increases their prices often rocket. When this happens, large increases in investment spending end up buying only small increases in capital goods, which determine how much output increases. In combination, these three distinct challenges—improving public investment, inducing private investment, and containing the price of capital goods—constitutes an agenda for overcoming the absorption problem. I think of them collectively as a strategy of "investing in investing." By that I mean that the society needs to spend money and expend effort to do what is necessary to reconcile increased investment with productive investment.

Improving Public Investment

Good public investment is the place to start. The government captures the revenues from natural resources and saves them, so it has the primary responsibility to prioritize their use. With business-as-usual, the likely outcome is that more will mean worse just through sliding further down the list of priorities.

If the government publicly decides to make a quantum leap in investment the outcome could be even worse than that. The political special-interest lobby groups that try to capture public spending are alerted that there is more money on the table and so exert themselves, through legitimate and illegitimate means. The resources burned up in such lobbying contests are called "rent-seeking." If rent-seeking is frustrated by checks and balances such as veto points, the lobbies may try to dismantle them. Nuhu's departure for Oxford was induced by effective lobbying, and dismantled one important check. Michael Ross, a political scientist from UCLA, aptly terms this higher-order destructiveness "rent-*seizing*." The experience that gave Ross that insight was not oil in Africa but timber in Thailand, where he documented the systematic dismantling of the checks which impeded the plunder of the country's forests.

But a decision for a quantum increase in public investment can also offer an opportunity to break with the past. Politically, it is easier to introduce new practices at a time of expansion than when budgets are flat. Within the public sector, investing in investing means a conscious strategy requiring two to three years to gear up: to recruit the staff and to introduce the decision procedures that would generate more productive projects.

Corruption in public-investment projects can be countered. The most elementary step is to subject all projects to competitive tendering. Although it is relatively easy to undermine competitive tendering through changes to the specifications of a contract, the corruption that ensues can be curbed. For example, a limit can be set on the value of changes to specifications that are permitted without high-level authorization. Multiple veto points can be built into that authorization process, mimicking at the level of the individual decision the macroeconomic results I discussed in chapter 3, where I suggested that in resource-rich countries veto points improved overall economic performance. As Nuhu's story illustrates, veto points are ultimately only robust if backed up by the threat of hard power: jail.

International action can reinforce these domestic steps: after all, many of the construction companies are international, headquartered in the OECD countries. International action has helped to address corruption in resource extraction through the Extractive Industries Transparency Initiative. The British government is now trying to do the same for construction through the Construction Sector Transparency Initiative. Among those who read *The Bottom Billion* and got in touch with me to offer help was an entrepreneur who ran a software company for the construction sector. I put him in contact with an African government which realized that standardizing the software used for state construction contracts would make it much easier to police corruption. Of course, corrupt companies and bribe-taking officials will eventually find ways around any particular defense. It helps to keep changing the locks.

The challenges of implementing a large public investment program go far beyond corruption. First, the program has to be designed: what should be included and what excluded? Both technically and politically this is difficult. Technically, how can the government work out the likely return on different investments and choose the best projects? The conventional answer has been to subject projects to the discipline of cost-benefit analysis. The technique has, however, been pretty useless in guiding public investment in low-income countries. (As the World Bank's new Director for Public Sector Policy recently admitted to me, "We know *that* doesn't work.") For the larger projects it misses out on many of the benefits because they accrue across the economy in ways that are immeasurable. The British government uses cost-benefit for many public investments, but it recognizes that the approach biases decisions away from the large, transformative investments such as intercity highways, or trunk roads. The *Standing Advisory Committee on Trunk Road Assessment* increases the estimated benefits of all trunk roads by 30 percent as an attempt to redress the bias. But 30 percent is completely arbitrary and may be inadequate. Guided by cost-benefit analysis, albeit with the 30 percent allowance, Britain lives in gridlock, lacking a network of fast trains and motorways that France, with its appetite for *les grands projets,* takes for granted.

Cost-benefit analysis is also impractical for most of the countries of the bottom billion because it requires the services of a small army of economists. The typical civil service has nowhere near the manpower to undertake such analysis except for a few large projects, and these are precisely the projects that are least suited to the technique. Even where there are sufficient technocrats to perform a cost-benefit analysis, their results are only as good as their independence. The typical government ministry in the societies of the bottom billion provides little protection for technocrats who cross the pet priorities of a minister. Yet countering politically driven priorities is half the purpose of cost-benefit analysis.

If investment should be determined neither by the whims of politicians nor the spurious precision of cost-benefit analysis, what should guide it? A more realistic approach for a low-income country might be to choose not Norway but some middle-income country as a role model. There are now plenty to choose from: societies such as Malaysia and Botswana that over the past three decades have successfully made the transition out of mass poverty and now offer modest comfort and hopeful prospects to ordinary citizens. From among these countries it should be possible to find one that, three decades ago, looked reasonably similar to any particular low-income country today. Since the role model middle-income country has successfully transformed its economy, public decisions on investment cannot have been too awful, and those that were major mistakes may serve as warnings. In other words, the pattern and sequence of investments taken by that society can be used as a template. A degree of prudence would suggest that rather than take one single country as a model the government might look at what was common in a few of them. The Growth Commission, which reported in 2008 under the leadership of Michael Spence, took precisely this pragmatic, learning-from-success approach. Spence asked what the thirteen formerly low-income countries that had achieved the feat of doubling their economies each decade for a generation had in common. One of them, which Spence regarded as critical, was indeed a sustained high rate of public investment.

Selecting the right public investments is a much more limited question than that posed by the Commission. Much of the public infrastructure needed for development lasts for decades, yet as a society transforms its needs may change quickly and drastically. The current infrastructure needs may be rural, yet if the society rapidly urbanizes, it will need urban transport systems. If these projects are delayed for too long they may have become too expensive to install. As I waited impatiently for my train to arrive on the London underground, a product of Victorian far-sightedness, my evident impatience was countered by a couple from New Zealand. "If only Auckland had an underground," one said. "We left it too late."

I will again turn to Nigeria, which is by far Africa's most populous country, and whose oil provides the society with an opportunity for transformation. Once that transformation happens, where will its people live? The question may sound too futuristic but actually we can answer it better than many questions with a much shorter horizon, such as what the oil price will be in twelve months. As Nigeria develops, its population will shift to the coastal cities. We can see this process already being played out on an even grander scale in China, as the population shifts by hundreds of millions from the interior.

Within a generation, Lagos, already the largest city in sub-Saharan Africa, will become a global megacity of over 20 million people. Already, it represents half of the entire non-oil economy of Nigeria, so that in the future, as oil runs down and is replaced by a new economy, most of it will be in Lagos and its environs. Lagos has two key advantages. One is that it is a port, and ports are key sites for global manufacturing. Not only does it help to be a port, it helps even more to be a large port.

The larger the city is, the more productive the people in it. The rule of thumb is that each time a city doubles in population, the productivity of its workers increases by around 6 percent. That might not sound a lot but if people move from hamlets to megacities the cumulative consequences can be substantial. Someone working in a city of 10 million is on average going to be 40 percent more productive than someone working in a city of 100,000—and most Africans currently live in places that are much smaller than that. The experience of China is so extraordinary that it might have no relevance for Africa: China's sheer size enables megacities to have large hinterlands but the same pattern is found in India. Africa needs more megacities. Tony Venables and I compared Africa's urbanization with that of India and found that Africa is missing out on productivity because it lacks cities like Mumbai. Lagos is Africa's best chance of a productive megacity.

If Nigeria's economic future lies in Lagos, and if that future could arrive within a generation—so long as the Nigerian government harnesses the nation's oil revenues—it is not difficult to work out where much of the public investment financed by oil should be located. Yet, paradoxically, Lagos is precisely, immaculately, the one place in Nigeria where oil money is not reaching.

To understand this paradox we have to turn to the politics of oil. Forty years ago, Nigeria fought a civil war over oil: the oil-rich region of the Niger Delta wanted to secede, and the other regions did not want to let it go. The political solution was to build a federal system with thirty-six states, among which half of the oil revenues are distributed. No one state is large enough to secede and, in any case, the local politicians get a constitutionally guaranteed share of the oil money. Lagos may be the future of the economy, but even its present prosperity is deeply resented by the other states. Its economy gives it a tax base and so the other states ganged up and voted that Lagos be constitutionally excluded from the oil revenue carve-up. This made some sense, at least within the Utilitarian calculus: Lagos is better off than other regions. But as a development strategy, the exclusion of Lagos is manifestly a denial of basic economic logic. Future opportunities are being sacrificed to the interests of the present. Investment can only produce a high return if it is put in the right place. The responsibility of the present generation of Nigerian adults to their children and grandchildren for the custody of the value of natural assets suggests that investment should be placed disproportionately in Lagos, not disproportionately elsewhere. Lagos is where many of those grandchildren will be living once the society has reached middle-income levels.

So far I have discussed how to plan public investment. But the best-laid plans still have to be put into practice. Corruption is not the only thing that can derail implementation: investment depends upon the coordination of a whole sequence of tasks. Soon after the onset of the first oil boom in 1975, the Nigerian government decided to invest heavily in infrastructure. This was very likely a sensible judgment. Thirty years later Tony Blair's Commission for Africa, directed by economist Nicholas Stern—also the author of the Stern Review of the Economics of Climate Change—reached the same conclusion: Africa's top priority was infrastructure.

While that initial prioritization was sound, the implementation went disastrously wrong. The government realized that a big push on infrastructure would require far more cement than Nigeria was currently producing. The proposed solution was to import cement. Officials were sent to the far corners of the earth to procure all the cement they could find. Without coordination, officials ordered cement deliverable at Lagos. Nobody, or at least nobody sufficiently senior, had thought through the critical path of constructing infrastructure. Cement is useless unless it can be unloaded from the ships that bring it. Lagos is a superb natural harbor; a whole fleet could rest safely at anchor there. But it lacks docks and cranes. As the queue of cement-laden ships lengthened and suppliers realized that the cement which they dispatched could not be unloaded for months or even years, they turned to the small print of their contracts. There sat a standard little clause referring to a concept with which most people outside the shipping business will be unfamiliar: demurrage. If a ship reaches its designated destination but cannot be unloaded within a set period, the buyer incurs a daily charge. Cement suppliers spotted that they were onto a good thing: find a ship that is due to be written off, fill it with cement, preferably cement that is cheap because of its inferior quality, and hope that the ship manages to make it to Lagos. Then leave it at anchor for as many years as possible, earning demurrage. Nigerians wryly refer to this episode as the Cement Armada. How much of it was due to corruption and how much to lack of coordination remains unclear. But it cautions against a "big push" surge in public investment.

As an investment project is implemented it needs to be supervised. The more politically or socially difficult the environment the more things are liable to go wrong and so the more supervision is needed. Over the years the World Bank has implemented several thousand development projects around the world, all of which are subsequently evaluated to see how well they worked out. Potentially, this massive data base might determine what increases a project's chances of success. With Lisa Chauvet and Marguerite Duponchel I decided to investigate it. The question we posed was what helped projects in the "fragile states" such as postconflict situations where the civil service has largely fallen apart. Unsurprisingly, projects were more likely to fail in such conditions. At issue was whether anything could be done about it. We found that World Bank supervision of projects was consistently more valuable in these conditions. Perhaps this provides some guide for resource-rich countries that want to scale up public investment but lack the manpower. Almost by definition, a resource-rich country is not going to get a lot of aid, or aid workers since agencies try to compensate for the inequities of natural-asset endowments by shifting aid to countries that are less fortunate. But the take-away here is not "rely on the World Bank," but "hire missing skills from abroad." Indeed, this was a key part of Botswana's strategy for harnessing its diamond revenues. The government was not too proud to recruit foreigners, both to train its own people, and to work with them in implementing its projects.

Encouraging Private Investment

The second part of the investing-in-investing agenda is to encourage private investment. At last we are getting into the comfort zone of most economists: since the 1980s the bulk of the profession has persuaded itself of the superiority of private action to public action. Applied to the harnessing of natural assets for development this found expression in two wild-seeming ideas.

One was to conclude that the rents from natural assets—in this case copper in Chile—were not worth the social costs of capturing. Leaving the rents with the resource-extraction companies would encourage investment in resource expansion and that would benefit the whole economy. Zambia copied this approach.

The other idea was that the government should indeed tax the rents from natural assets but then give them back. In principle it could literally hand the money to ordinary citizens, except that politicians will do that only as a last resort. Faced by open insurrection in the oil-producing region of the Delta, in October 2009 the government of Nigeria announced that it would distribute 10 percent of oil revenues directly to households living there. Currently there is no indication as to how it will actually administer such a distribution. Usually, the more practical solution is for the government to channel the money back to private business through the banking system. The hope is that private business will do a better job of investment than the government. This was the approach followed by the government of Kazakhstan: rather than increase public investment it placed much of the money in the local banks which then lent it on to businesses, while the rest of the money it saved abroad following the Norwegian model.

The global economic crisis has taken the shine off the magic of the market, although the bulk of the economics profession remains in denial. But what was the outcome of the application to the domestic investment of resource revenues? For some years Kazakhstan appeared to be a dizzying success. Then it crashed disastrously. The local banks had geared up the natural-resource money by borrowing internationally, using the government's prudent savings abroad as an implicit collateral. What had those wise businessmen done with the money they borrowed from the banks? The answer was property. Kazakhstan enjoyed a property bonanza to end all property bonanzas. If you live in America or Britain you will now know why such investment is not necessarily smart. Private investors can blunder just as badly as government, and when their errors are collectively catastrophic the government has to bail them out. So, while it makes sense to share the investment effort with the private sector, there is a strong case for balance. The public sector should not abrogate its responsibilities to private actors.

Nevertheless, there is much that the government can do to encourage private investment. If the policy environment is dysfunctional, an increase in public investment can potentially be offset by a hemorrhage of private wealth abroad through capital flight. This is precisely what happened during the first oil boom in Nigeria: public investment rose, albeit very wastefully through mistakes such as the Cement Armada, but private investment fell as people moved wealth out of the country.

One obvious opportunity for private investment is in the resource-extraction sector itself. Resource extraction is usually very capital-intensive and thus too costly for the government of a low-income country to finance. For that reason the sector usually does not provide many jobs. More fundamentally, since investment in extraction accelerates the depletion of natural assets, it brings closer the day when the society must live on the revenue from some other activity. So investment in resource extraction may yield big numbers but it is not sufficient to be transformative.

Despite high returns, aside from resource extraction, private investment has been limited. One likely reason is that resource-rich economies are volatile: as the economy lurches from boom to bust businesses face too much uncertainty. So policies that could soften the shocks should help to promote private investment. Indeed, this was one rationale for the Fund's recommendation for saving resource revenues abroad. However, from the perspective of investment that approach throws out the baby with the bathwater.

With what now looks like foresight—but was entirely fortuitous—Benedikt and I decided to investigate how to cushion crashes.

Typically, when the world prices of commodities drop, the low-income commodity exporters go into a severe bust during which output falls across the economy.

Two types of domestic policies might help to mitigate crashes. One consists of *responses* to the crash, of the type with which we have all now become familiar. Getting the responses right is intrinsically dicey: the right response is controversial and in any case it requires the government to act in a timely fashion. The other type is *structural*. It consists of policies that can be put in place prior to the crash and simply left there. We decided that because this type of policy demanded less of government, research on it might potentially be more helpful to the countries of the bottom billion.

There are currently several international surveys that assess government policies for investment. A useful one is the annual *Doing Business* survey, produced by the World Bank. Whereas other surveys are based mostly on opinions, this one is based on objective measures, such as the number of days it takes for goods to clear customs, or the number of permits that are needed before a new business can legally be opened. We decided to use this data to investigate whether anything could mitigate output losses in commodity-exporting countries following a price crash.

The number from the *Doing Business* survey that usually gets reported is a summary measure produced by averaging many underlying indicators. We started with that summary measure and then drilled down to see which components were actually crucial. We came down to a core of indicators all clustered around the speed with which businesses could be opened and closed. The more conducive the policies to flexibility the smaller the output losses from any given hit from a drop in export earnings.

Although our results were statistical, they made some intuitive sense. A crash in commodity prices shifts opportunities within the economy. Some activities need to contract but others should expand. If expansion is frustrated, output loss is accentuated. However, even impeding contraction can be detrimental: while unviable firms linger in limbo their resources cannot be deployed more productively. So the policy message was clear enough: the governments of commodity-exporting countries should set policies that made it as easy as possible to open and close businesses.

Our next question was whether they were doing that already. As far as we could tell the reality was precisely the opposite: the countries that stood to gain most from flexible business environments were the least likely to have them. Presumably, underlying this perverse relationship is a dysfunctional political economy. Resource revenues interfere with the normal process whereby politicians deliver those policies that are particularly suited to the society. An implication is that the governments of resource-rich countries could do considerably better in setting policies conducive to diversified private investment.

We next investigated whether the international community could do anything that would mitigate the adverse consequences of commodity shocks through aid. As with domestic policies, aid is part *response* and part *structural*. Response is much more demanding, and given the sclerotic way in which aid is organized, unrealistic. By the time donors have responded to a crash in commodity prices it is history. So we focused on the structural. Although aid is currently subject to much criticism, we found that structural aid indeed helps to soften the adverse effects of commodity shocks. Yet we could find no tendency for aid agencies to target funds toward the most shock-prone low-income societies. Such differential vulnerability did not seem to be taken into account. Therefore while smart responses are hit or miss, both domestic and international policies can consistently ease commodity crashes if guided toward the structural.

Bringing Down the Price of Capital Goods

During the recent commodity boom most co...
ing countries experienced property booms. Cor...
the property booms were construction booms. In tu...
struction booms drove up the cost of construction. For...
in Nigeria construction costs soared in just a few yea...
cost of construction rose fourfold relative to the prices of o...
goods and services. So Nigerians may have spent a lot more o...
investment, but actually not bought much more with it. The...
increases did not translate into an equivalent amount of extra
capital. Since both the government and private investors need
construction, the problem of high costs is common to both,
and undoes both public and private increases in spending on
investment.

The final part of the investing-in-investing agenda is to make
sure that extra spending on investment gets as much bang for the
buck as possible rather than being dissipated in high costs. What,
practically, can a government do? We might start by recalling the
steps involved in constructing a new building. First, you need
the land. In many of the countries of the bottom billion there is
no proper land market: rights are confused and contested, or the
government claims to own all the land but has no proper pro-
cedure for allocating it. Most construction is occurring in urban
areas, thus the priority is to clarify the rights to land and facilitate
the development of a market. Sierra Leone is a postconflict country which has just discovered oil. Its capital, Freetown, should
be in the throes of a construction boom, yet there is not a crane
in sight. During the years of political chaos many competing
claims on urban land were registered. Until these are reconciled
by the sclerotic courts construction is stalled. Once you have the

, you need permission to build, giving some bureaucrat the opportunity to extract a bribe. The government can make the planning process quicker, less discretionary, and more transparent. Construction requires special skills. In a society where there has been little investment for decades these skills will be in short supply once investment is scaled up. So expanding the training of construction workers can help. Finally, those Nigerian public officials got it right in 1975: construction means cement. But imports need good port facilities and domestic production needs good transport arteries. Recently, while visiting the Nigerian Minister of Industries I was introduced to the richest man in Nigeria (which means very rich indeed). He proved a disarmingly down-to-earth person who made his fortune by recognizing that cement was going to be the bottleneck; he sells it at around double the world price.

The capital goods needed for investment are partly structures and partly equipment: roads and trucks. The countries of the bottom billion import equipment rather than producing it domestically, yet prices are nevertheless systematically above world levels. Since this again reduces the value of investment spending, Tony and I tried to find out what was causing it. We found that market size matters: the combination of small economies and low rates of investment imply that the market for any particular type of equipment is probably tiny, and therefore likely to be exploited by monopolies and cartels. Fortunately, to an extent this problem is self-correcting. Whereas an increase in investment spending accentuates the problem of expensive construction, it should reduce the problem of expensive equipment. However, these automatic effects can be reinforced by policies that will help enlarge the market. The most straightforward way is to coordinate with neighboring countries, removing the barriers to region-wide marketing of imported equipment. Recently, while in Sierra Leone I was interviewed by a local journalist. The interview over, I turned the tables. It transpired that he was both journalist and entrepreneur, having established his own newspaper. Building up a newspaper had not been easy, most particularly because of the difficulty of finding affordable printing machinery. In order to track down the appropriate secondhand equipment he had needed to travel to Nigeria, the only significant market in West Africa. Visas, foreign currency, and the lack of transport connections had all impeded the transaction, but what saved the day was that some of the Nigerian banks had established a regional network with branch offices in Sierra Leone.

Seizing the Slump

The resource-rich countries have just lived through the biggest bonanza they have ever experienced. A bonanza is precisely the wrong time to gain attention for the investing-in-investing agenda: governments are awash with money, and that same spirit of irrational exuberance that proved so disastrous in the richest societies pervades discussion in the poorest. The bonanza is over: boom-time has given way to slump-time. Yet, paradoxically, now is the moment for investing in investing. The salutary knowledge that a huge opportunity may have been missed concentrates minds. The investing-in-investing agenda does not itself require large increases in spending; it is the prelude to ramping up investment. Without it an investment boom would be unlikely to translate into sustainably higher growth. And so the slump is itself an opportunity to be seized before the next boom comes along.

Nature as a Factory

CHAPTER 8

Is a Fish a Natural Asset?

OIL, COPPER, AND ALL THE OTHER MINERALS can only be used once: they are intrinsically depleting natural assets. But nature is also a factory, able to continue production indefinitely. This natural process of production is, of course, *re*production: fish, trees, pandas are all capable of reproducing (although pandas do not seem to be very good at it). Such renewable natural assets are a double blessing. We did not create them and yet we can harvest them for eternity.

The menace of plunder is even starker with renewable natural assets than it was with depletable natural assets. The peculiar vulnerability of reproduction compared to other processes of production is that the continued flow of consumable goods depends upon the maintenance of a massive stock of them. If cars were produced in the same way as wood, General Motors would need a stock of many times its annual production from which to cull its new cars. Instead, it just needs a factory. Plundering a factory is not nearly as enticing as plundering a huge stock of the output. The incentive for the plunder of reproduction is therefore acute. We are able to enjoy the harvest from reproducible natural assets because previous generations refrained from such plunder. They did not exhaust the stock and so infringe the rights of future generations. What was the man who shot the last dodo thinking at the time? Perhaps not very much more than "got it!"; perhaps that since it was the last one it could not breed; or perhaps he did not realize that it was the last one until it was too late. Instinctively we sense that plundering a renewable natural asset to extinction seems an appalling error. Can economics add anything useful to such sentiments?

In the simplest economies everything is sustainable: the economy remains exactly the same from one year to the next. This is not a world that we should necessarily aspire to. If everything stays the same, that includes the desperate poverty of the bottom billion. Nor is it now feasible: those nonrenewable assets are gradually running out. But in such an economy the natural world reproduces itself, year-in, year-out, and keeps precisely the same value. A fish this year is worth the same as a fish next year. If the natural assets maintain their value, the return on them is simply their physical rate of reproduction: trees grow at a certain rate per year, fish have offspring.

In a world that is growing and changing, the renewable natural assets may become more or less abundant relative to the other goods. In nineteenth-century Australia, the rabbits introduced from England bred so profusely that they switched from being an asset to a pest; their value actually dropped below zero. In the twenty-first century, seafood, which is a luxury, will become radically more valuable even if we harvest it so as to maintain the stock constant. The same number of lobsters is going to have to be shared among many more people. In this world, the one in which we live, the prices of renewable assets change.

The Hotelling Rule dictates that if nonrenewable natural assets are depleted at a socially efficient rate their price, or more properly that part of their price constituted by the rent, should rise at the world rate of interest. If the price rises more rapidly than that we are over-exploiting. If we left more of the stuff in the ground the return on it would exceed the return on other types of investment. The equivalent socially efficient exploitation for a renewable natural asset is that the *total* return should equal the world interest rate. The total return on a renewable natural asset has two components: the rate of reproduction plus any change in the price. Complicated as this may sound, it is worth hanging on to, because it gives us a benchmark for the responsible use of a renewable natural asset.

Once we apply this rule it is apparent that literal sustainability—the precise maintenance of the stock of renewable natural assets—is not a sensible goal. There is no necessary economic virtue in maintaining the natural world in the style to which it has become accustomed. In medieval Britain the government worried that there would not be enough yew wood for longbows and so planted trees in all village churchyards. They still look pretty but we no longer need the wood; thanks to technology we can now shoot people more efficiently. Nevertheless, the maintenance of the stock of a renewable asset does have some ethical significance, in that it gives us a foothold in the slippery terrain of what is a responsible rate of harvest for which we do not need to compensate the future. Natural assets are for us to use, but "us" includes the rights of future generations. As with other natural assets, the future has rights to them because these assets are not man-made and thus the present generation only has custodial rights of usage.

Recall that with nonrenewable natural assets the responsibility of custody required us to bequeath to future generations an asset of equal value to that we had depleted. How are things different with a renewable asset? The ethical difference is that a renewable asset automatically generates output each year—the natural harvest. This is ours to consume, just as it was for our ancestors. We do not need to compensate the future for consuming this sustainable harvest of natural assets; the future will be able to do the same. This is what we are entitled to take, but nevertheless it may not be the smartest rate of harvest. If we consume seafood at the rate which keeps the stock constant, so that only the same amount of seafood can be consumed each year, its price will rocket. So the return on investing in an increased stock of seafood is likely to be much higher than for most other forms of investment. As a society we are not *obliged* to do this for the future; our government does not have to hand over to some future government this enhanced stock of seafood as a social asset. It would simply be a smart form of private investment, the sort of investment, which, as long as the property rights are sorted out, you would want your pension fund to put its money into. The future has a right to the same number of lobsters as we have, for free, but if it wants more than that at our expense, it will need to compensate us for all those delicious lobsters that we have left in the sea in order to increase the stock. So, the sustainability of seafood stocks is not the ideal strategy. We have a right to eat the physically sustainable off-take, but we would be smart to let some of those lobsters breed instead of eating them, selling them to the future for a good price.

What Will the Future Think of Us?

Lobsters are an uncomplicated example (unless you are a member of the Lobster Liberation Front which, incidentally, is a genuine organization). They are a luxury and we should only forego eating some of the sustainable harvest in favor of that greedier, richer future if it pays us handsomely for our restraint.

Now let's take an emotionally more troubling case: forests. Is requiring our generation to sustain the world's forests setting the ethical bar too high? Of course we now know that forests are a handy way of storing carbon, but I want to defer thinking about carbon until the next chapter. Instead I would ask you to think back a couple of decades to the ethics of forest management before we realized that global warming was going to be a problem. Should all forests be preserved? Clearly, our ancestors did not think so. They built the cities where we live, and the farms on which we grow our food, on land that had previously been covered in trees. Ethically, depleting a renewable asset must meet the same test as depleting a nonrenewable asset: the responsibility of custody requires that those future generations should say to us, "Yes, that's fine; you have fully compensated us with other assets." Of course, in a literal sense we will never know. We will be dead and gone by the time the future passes judgment on us. We must therefore resort to the standard technique used by moral philosophers for thinking through an ethical problem: a *thought experiment.*

In this instance the thought experiment is quite straightforward. We simply need to put ourselves in the shoes of future citizens. What would they regard as ethically justifiable behavior on the part of the present generation? Two conditions must jointly hold before it is ethically justifiable for the present generation to deplete a forest. One is that there are other investment opportunities opened up by cutting the forest that yield a higher return than the *total* return on the forest. Since the total return on a renewable asset includes the appreciation in the price of the asset, if wood gradually gets more valuable we have to take that into account in deciding whether or not to cut down the forest now. The other condition is that we actually do bequeath all these other investments to the future as socially owned assets.

If we cut down the last tree, or eat the last fish, will our descendants curse us for depriving them of their patrimony? Even if we could teleport ourselves physically into the future, putting ourselves in the position of the future offers a better ethical guide. The attitude of future citizens may be warped because they know less than we do. Even if we ate the last fish, our descendants might merely shrug and say, "Never mind, we would not have liked fish anyway." We know better: how could a person who has never had a fish know what they are missing? Alternatively, their actual judgment of the past plunder of natural assets may be too harsh.

Here is an example. The current generation of Eritreans curse the past for the plunder of the country's trees. More specifically, Eritreans blame the current lack of trees on Ethiopians, accusing them of plunder during the decades when the two countries were united. Following independence the Eritrean government undertook a massive replanting campaign of 5 million trees; the forests are being re-established. But Eritrea has an unusually complicated colonial history and in fact had already been through virtually the same psychology of grievance before. Prior to being part of Ethiopia, Eritrea had been a colony of Italy. During the Ethiopian period the explanation for the lack of trees was that the Italians had plundered them. As with the current government, blaming the previous colonizer had obvious advantages. Nor is that the end of the blame chain. Although Eritrea has a complicated colonial history, it was a relatively brief one. Italy was late on the scene in the scramble for Africa and Eritrea was the last place left to grab. As those first Italian colonizers scanned the terrain around the turn of the twentieth century one disappointing feature was the near absence of trees. Although the Italians could scarcely mistake the fact that they were unwelcome, the lack of trees provided an ethical fig-leaf of justification for colonization: indeed a whole fig-forest. The reason there were no trees must be that the inhabitants had plundered them. Colonization could proceed in good conscience, secure in the knowledge that a custodial role was needed.

Blame has echoed down the decades, hijacked by whoever held power to justify their dominion over those they had vanquished. You may be wondering how far back it goes. At the bottom of the archives, so to speak, is a travel narrative from the early sixteenth century, written by a monk who had journeyed through the country and written down his impressions. Mainly his comments were about people, but he noted one peculiar feature of the landscape: the absence of trees.

So is the story of plunder a complete fiction? Not quite: squeezed in between the Italians and the Ethiopians was a brief period of British occupation. As Michaela Wrong describes in *I Didn't Do It for You*, the British inadvertently liberated Eritrea from the Italians during the Second World War as a result of the North African campaign. The British temporarily governed a country in which they had no long-term interest, and they were in the middle of fighting a war that was going badly. As part of the war effort they needed wood and so chopped down what they could find. Most of Eritrea is too dry to sustain tree growth, but there were pockets of forest, and these were plundered. But for once there were no kudos in blaming the British: they were the liberators so no blame was assigned them.

So how the future regards our actions will perhaps depend not just on what we have done, but on what it is convenient for the future to remember. In the end, however, what it thinks of us is of no consequence; the ethical benchmark should be how it would see us were it in full command of the facts. The thought experiment is not just more feasible than teleporting into the future, it is also more pertinent.

The Right to Fish

So far I have skated over the distinction between private ownership and social ownership. It is now time to turn to the question which forms the title of this chapter: is a fish a natural asset? A defining feature of a *natural* asset is that it is not man-made. So is a fish man-made? Some are and some are not. If you buy smoked salmon in a supermarket you will have noticed that there are two types: wild and farmed. A farmed salmon is no more a natural asset than is a cow. It has been bred and reared by means of human technology and capital. Only wild fish are natural assets. The same applies to trees. If you plant an orchard it is not a natural asset; it is your private investment. Trees are natural assets only when they have not been planted by human effort and are on land that is not privately owned. The planting and the ownership are linked; people will not bother to plant trees on land that they do not own. Near where I live is a street that became a cause célèbre in British social history. Initially, all the houses were privately owned, but then social housing was constructed. So outraged were the older residents by the intrusion of poorer people that the local authority built a wall across the street. Like the Berlin Wall, this wall eventually came down, and under Mrs. Thatcher the public housing was sold to private buyers. But the street's history of division is still visible, now more than ever: in the half which has always been private the front gardens are now dominated by mature trees, but not in the half that was tenanted. Without ownership, people are not willing to invest in immovable assets.

Recall the fate of the buffalo: those assets not privately owned and easily found are vulnerable. Until recently wild fish had natural protection by being hidden in the sea. Indeed, as more were caught their natural protection intensified because they became harder to find. But advances in fishing technology have radically changed the sustainability of wild fish. They can now be depleted so effectively that the few remaining become unviable. By the time that the stock of fish is reduced to the point at which mankind cannot find any more, the fish cannot find each other: reproduction ceases. Until recently the wild forests of the Amazon had natural protection because the wood and the land were not sufficiently valuable to warrant being cut down. No more. The government opened up the land for private farming. Economists refer to this as the "common pool" problem, or the "tragedy of the commons." In the absence of private property rights all natural assets are liable to be plundered unless defended by local social conventions, and such conventions do not usually survive rapid social change. The plunder of renewable assets is even more of a disaster than that of nonrenewables. When a renewable asset becomes extinct not just some future generation, but *every* future generation is deprived of its rights.

Where does all this leave us? We have a benchmark of socially efficient management of renewable assets: the harvest from a natural asset should evolve such that its value appreciates over the years sufficiently for the total return—the appreciation plus the harvest—to equal the return on other assets. We have an ethical rule for responsible custody. The sustainable harvest is ours for the taking, but we can deviate in either direction: building the stock but making the future pay, or depleting it and providing the future with compensation. Finally, we have a tension between the need for natural assets to be socially owned—they belong to all of us, including future generations—and the need for them to be protected from plunder. In chapter 2 I argued that the most reasonable place to lodge the rights to natural assets is with governments. The planet is divided into countries, each with a recognized government that in principle can represent the collective interests of its citizens. This works for most natural assets but not for all of them. The high seas are not assigned to any nation, and so the rights to the fish in them should accrue to the entire world population: they are a global public good. Similarly, the polar territories are not assigned to any nation. Rights over them are currently contested. This brings us back to the proximity principle. We feel greater obligations to people who are proximate to us. We also feel we have greater rights to natural assets that are proximate to us. The nations that border on the Arctic—Canada, Norway, and Russia—are all claiming ownership of its natural assets. The issue has come to a head now that it seems likely that there are 90 billion barrels of oil to be exploited. By analogy, should the high seas be assigned to whichever country is closest to them, so that all fish become owned by some national government? Currently, there are three classes of fish and ownership: those that are farmed are the property of the fish farm; those in territorial waters are the property of some government; and those beyond territorial waters are ownership-free. There is nothing intrinsic to a fish which makes it a natural asset; it simply depends where it is.

For those fish living within territorial waters it is the responsibility of government both to capture value for the society as a whole and to protect the rights of future generations. Both require that the government limit the catch by creating rights to a particular quantity of fish, enforced by policing. These rights—fishing quotas—are valuable, so who should get that value? To my mind the answer to this is straightforward: the rights should accrue to citizens. They don't. Instead they have been captured by the fishing lobby. The idea that fishermen should get the rights to scarce fish for free is analogous to oil companies getting the rights to oil for free. It creates a destructive dynamic. Should the quotas be handed out for free the lobbies will want more of them. Fishermen should have a strong interest in restricting the catch, for if the fish run out their jobs will disappear and their boats become worthless. If a valuable social asset is being handed out for free I would want as much of it as I could possibly get. Were quotas auctioned to fishermen, as oil rights are auctioned to oil companies, there would be far less pressure to expand the quotas. But as it is, fishermen lobby very effectively. As a result, politicians have conceded unsustainable harvest rates. Indeed, the fishing lobby has surpassed itself. Not only does it get its quotas for free, it receives large subsidies as well.

The world fish catch is of the order of $80 billion annually. World fishing subsidies are of the order of $30 billion. The subsidies are, of course, for the fishing fleets of the rich countries of the OECD. But they subsidize the activities of these fleets wherever they choose to sail. If their activities were confined to the territorial waters of the OECD then at least OECD taxpayers would be financing the plunder of their own future. As it is, the fleets are subsidized to catch fish both in international waters and in the ill-defended waters of the bottom billion. The Minister for Fisheries in Sierra Leone explained the problem. The government lacks the means to police its territorial waters and so its fishermen must watch, helpless, while subsidized foreign boats deplete the fish stock. The only assistance has come from the Chinese government which provided a police vessel. Ironically, the first fishing boat it managed to arrest was Chinese. Sierra Leone at least has a Minister of Fisheries; but Somalia does not even have a government. Its undefended coastal waters have been ransacked by foreign fleets, mostly subsidized. As local Somali fishermen watched their livelihoods snatched from them they heeded some age-old advice and became fishers of men.

Unsurprisingly, given these remarkably misaligned incentives, the world's fishing fleet is estimated to be 40 percent larger than warranted by a sustainable catch. And recall, even a sustainable catch may be too large, given that stocks should be growing to meet the appetites of the future. The withdrawal of subsidies is a collective action problem. No individual OECD government wants to put its national fleet at a disadvantage relative to others. Yet the OECD has been dealing with such challenges of coordination for decades. The appropriate body is the World Trade Organization which could orchestrate a gradual but binding mutual de-escalation of subsidies.

Giving away valuable fishing quotas not only compounds the dysfunctional incentives provided by subsidies, it brings the risk of corruption. In Iceland, the value of fish quotas is big relative to other assets. Iceland is currently better known for its banks than for its fish: it led the world on financial catastrophe. There is a link. The original collateral the banks used to expand consisted of those fish quotas. The natural assets which should have accrued to ordinary Icelanders were politically misappropriated, yet those same ordinary Icelanders now own the man-made liabilities that the banks ran up on the back of those natural assets.

Why are fish quotas given away? One explanation may be that the right to catch fish was not always valuable. There were plenty of fish in the sea because technology was so primitive: the value of a fish accrued from the dangerous work of catching it. In this respect fishing was analogous to coal mining. Coal was abundant but difficult to extract, thus most of its value accrued from that task rather than from the possession of the right to extract. That remains true for coal, but not for fish. Advances have already lowered the cost of fishing, and prospective technologies will sweep fish up with even greater efficiency. As a result, if fish are left unowned they will be plundered to extinction.

The dynamics of that plunder are analogous to a gold rush, and with all of its inefficiency. Initially, the same boats, now equipped with new technology, catch more fish and so become super-profitable. More boats are built. These extra boats crowd in on already depleted fishing grounds and so the catch of each boat is reduced again until the extraordinary profits have disappeared. We end up in an equilibrium that is inefficient: boats that are far less productive than they could have been because fish are so scarce. What has happened is that the technological advance had made fish less like coal and more like oil. The rights to extraction became valuable because the commodity was worth more than the cost of getting it. In economic terms the technological advance created rents on fish. But then, because of the lack of ownership rights over those rents they became dissipated by the costs incurred in rent-seeking. Too many boats crowded in, just like the thousands of hopeful young men in Sierra Leone who crowd in to seek alluvial diamonds.

But unlike gold and diamonds, fish are a renewable asset. Their over-exploitation plunders the future much more spectacularly by driving stocks below the point at which they can reproduce. Despite the diminishing stock, fishermen do not make fortunes. Theirs remains a tough and chancy profession. But if quotas are introduced those rents do not get dissipated by too many boats chasing too few fish. Those with the quotas can now catch valuable fish at low cost; the value of the natural asset is the value of these rents. Fishermen may feel that they have always had the right to catch fish and so the entitlements to the quotas should be theirs. But the fishermen only had the right to fish while fish had little value as a natural asset. Again, the value accrued from their efforts. That is the right they continue to have: to a decent return on their effort. They have the right neither to plunder the future, as in a free-for-all, nor to the rents created by limiting the catch.

A government should manage its rights over unassigned renewable natural assets within its territory. With fish it should auction them to fishermen. If local fishermen want to buy them they should pay a competitive price; otherwise other citizens are being plundered.

The cost of policing a quota sometimes depends upon the cooperation of locals. In this case it might therefore be sensible to let the locals keep at least some of the rents. Such is the case with wild forests. If the government attempts to keep all the rents, locals will resort to illicit felling and poaching.

Some governments have attempted to counter this by creating game parks from which the local inhabitants are removed. This is the model of national parks in the United States, where it generally worked because the policy was introduced before they had a significant resident population. In Tanzania and other long-populated countries, it is a different matter. It turns out that the total exclusion of inhabitants is not even environmentally efficient. The people excluded from the park shift their exploitation to neighboring areas, so while the harvest of renewable assets within the Park drops to zero, that in the neighboring areas is increased. In most ecosystems damage increases more than proportional to the harvest: it is better to spread the harvest evenly over a large area than have part of it fully protected and the other part plundered. Total exclusion is a bureaucratic response to sustainability rather than an economic one. It is better to allow the local population to exploit the habitat, assigning to it the rights to the value of the natural assets. The more localized such rights the more the solution approaches turning natural assets into private property. A privately owned forest, like a privately owned fish farm, has a greater incentive to manage the asset sustainably. The objection to handing natural assets over as private property is that other citizens, present and future, are being plundered of their rights. But if the cost of enforcing social rights over renewable natural assets exceeds their value, privatizing them for free is far better than leaving them unprotected. While it might appear that privatization robs other citizens, it actually prevents the asset from being plundered to extinction.

A Modest Proposal

The most vulnerable natural assets of all are fish that swim in international waters. They are currently the equivalent of the buffalo, with only weak international protection. Fortunately, most fish need coastal waters and these are within the 200 miles of territorial rights. The open oceans are the equivalent of deserts and only around 15 percent of the global fish catch comes from them, worth about $12 billion. Once fleets had slimmed down to an efficient level, the rents from catching these fish are estimated as somewhere in the wide range of 10–50 percent, implying a total of between $1.2 and $6 billion. These rents are currently being dissipated in the costs of an over-large world fleet. Instead, they should be captured by society.

One approach would be to extend national waters so that every drop of every ocean belonged to some nation or other. Although the rents from international fish are not massive, such an extension of national rights would set a very costly precedent. Once the waters were assigned to nations, the ocean floor beneath them would surely follow. Technology will soon open up the exploitation of its minerals. Already oil and gold are being extracted from beneath deep water. This would be a radical over-extension of the principle of geographic proximity, which is in any case a pretty weak principle. Political geography is not a continuum: national borders are cliff edges. Within those borders citizens have equal rights and, as redistributive taxation demonstrates, they have strong claims upon each other. Beyond national borders people's rights and claims are far weaker. Further, carving up the oceans according to the principle of proximity would create the equivalent of a few countries like Kuwait. The new Kuwaits would be the small, remote islands in the middle of the oceans, able to lay claim to huge tracts of the planet and the resulting rights to natural assets such as fish and minerals. The principle of proximity to the sea would systematically exclude the world's poorest people, namely those living in landlocked countries. All property rights to natural assets are artificial constructs. It bears repeating: since they are not created, natural assets have no natural owners.

A better approach would be to assign the natural assets of the oceans to the United Nations. As a world organization the UN is far from ideal, but we are unlikely to find one more appropriate. The protection of wild fish means setting and enforcing limits on the catch. Some entity has to set these limits, and with that elusive combination of custody and investment acumen. As the limits bite, the entitlements to catch fish become valuable. If these entitlements are just *given* to those who catch fish, the political dynamic can becomes disastrous: each fishing nation will focus its lobbying efforts on getting as large an entitlement as possible. In economic terminology, there are too many externalities. The benefits to society as a whole are not aligned with the interests of those with the power of decision. To internalize these externalities, which means to align incentives with the social interest, the value of the entitlements should accrue to the entity setting the rules. In a fish farm this happens automatically: the owner of the fish farm takes out only the number of fish that is consistent with long-term profit maximization. The miracle of the market is that his interest is aligned with ours. He makes money by providing us with what we want.

By assigning the rights over the oceans to the United Nations the high seas would, in effect, be turned into a giant fish farm. The bare minimum would be for the United Nations to limit the harvest to a scientifically determined sustainable rate; that which would keep the stock constant. But of course the price of fish is likely to rise as the world gets richer and more populous. So building up the fish stock is a good investment. The UN would need not only scientists to advise on the physically sustainable rate of harvest, but economists who might, for example, propose an initially lower rate that would enable the stock to grow. Potentially, the UN could even borrow on the collateral of its fish rights. It would be a better cause than that of the Icelandic banks.

As the owner of the fish stock, the United Nations would face the right incentives to maximize long-term social value by limiting the permitted annual harvest, auctioning off the rights to the permitted amount each year. The challenge would be how to enforce these limits on the number of fish caught. Though the obvious place for enforcement might appear to be where fish are caught, policing the oceans is a massive task, even with satellites. The easiest point at which to police fishing limits may be where they are landed, or where they are priced: the wholesale markets through which almost all deep-sea fish must pass before reaching your table. The United Nations would auction the quota rights to traders who would then on-sell them in each wholesale market. Analogous to a tax, a wholesale transaction of fish would be legal only if attached to the appropriate quantity of quota rights. These quota rights would trade on a world market. For all practical purposes the system would be like an international tax. A consumer buying a fish would know how much she had paid to the United Nations. Because people do not like paying taxes this would create a healthy dynamic: the tax payer would ask both why the tax was necessary and what the United Nations was doing with the money. The United Nations could do with a dose of taxpayer scrutiny

The group that will object most to this suggestion, of course, is the fishing lobby. The basis for its objection will be, quite simply, that it wants to keep the rents from a natural asset to itself. But again: why should fishermen own the rights resulting from natural scarcity? When fish were sufficiently abundant that the catch was well below the sustainable rate, the total value in a fish brought to market was the result of the effort involved in catching it. There were no rents in fishing. But as fish became scarce and so in one sense harder to catch, less of the value was due to the catching and more due to possession of the *right* to catch.

Since more people want to catch fish than can be allowed to do so, there is no rationale for giving the right away to fishermen through political patronage. The value of those rents should accrue to all of us.

But who is "us"? The oceans are not national territory; they are the true global dominion of mankind. And as renewable natural assets, wild fish belong to future generations as much as they do to us. Beyond that sustainable rate of harvest, we are guilty of plunder unless we compensate the future with assets that it would accept as equivalent value. For all its faults the United Nations is more deserving of these rents than any of the other likely recipients. It provides global public goods, such as the World Food Programme, which nobody in particular wants to pay for: the intrinsic problem with public goods is free-riding. Paying for the emergency relief that prevents starvation by a global tax on fish may seem unlikely, but would actually link two important global needs. The World Food Programme would have a reliable income stream and thus be better able to meet acute needs; the fishing industry would have a viable future; consumers would know that the fish they were eating were not the product of plunder. It would even be good for fish.

CHAPTER 9

Natural Liabilities

FACTORIES PRODUCE THE GOODS THAT WE WANT. They also spew out smoke. The smoky factory is, in fact, the classic image used by economists to illustrate the idea of an externality. The factory sells the goods but does not have to pay for the smoke. We now know that smoke is more damaging than previously appreciated. There is nothing more natural than carbon dioxide; it is one of the basic ingredients of life. Yet carbon has become a natural liability. It accumulates up in the atmosphere, trapping in heat. Of course carbon only becomes a problem when it passes the threshold at which it is excessive. We have passed that threshold.

As the extra carbon traps in heat, the world heats up, and as it heats up the climate becomes more volatile. The consequences are wide-ranging, but Africa will be the region most severely affected. Africa is huge and climate change will not affect it uniformly, but it seems likely that the drier parts will become drier still, making staple foods unviable. Increased climate variation, which means droughts, floods, and bouts of intense heat, can wreak havoc with traditional cultivation. Agriculture, which is currently Africa's main economic activity, will become less productive. A rapidly growing population will be scratching a living from a progressively less amenable natural environment.

Carbon brings together the key themes of this book. Although it is natural, extra carbon is now a liability; there is nothing intrinsically benign about nature. It is emitted not just by industry but by a number of natural processes. For example, probably the most natural of all human economic activities is rearing cattle. Pastoralists have been ranging the wilderness for millennia. Unfortunately, in terms of global warming, they are more of a menace than nuclear power stations, which produce energy without emitting carbon. That is because cows fart.

Being renewable, carbon shares much of the economics of fish and trees, except that instead of being a renewable natural asset it is a renewable natural liability. The damage it does depends not upon how much is emitted today, but on how much has been emitted cumulatively over recent decades. Because it accumulates in the atmosphere, it has to be thought of as a stock as well as a flow. Indeed, carbon is the natural equivalent of a debt. Excess carbon builds up in the atmosphere the same way borrowing builds up in the bank. A debt is simply a negative asset, thus everything that I have said about the depletion of assets applies equally to the accumulation of debts. These are natural liabilities which future generations will have to meet, and so we have a responsibility to give the future due consideration when we decide whether to accumulate them.

Natural liabilities also share that distinctive feature of a natural asset: a lack of natural owners. There is no clear way of assigning them to specific debtors. The key difference is that in the absence of natural owners, people are only too keen to muscle in with claims on natural assets, whereas natural liabilities are nature's orphans. The Inuit are not agitating to own the carbon above their heads, only the oil beneath their feet.

The lack of natural owners for natural assets leads to plunder. The lack of natural owners for natural liabilities produces plunder in a different form: liabilities are run up as long as in the process some private gain accrues. There is no reason to think that the private gains will be larger than the social losses.

Natural assets intrinsically require a high degree of social cooperation, which markets cannot provide until ownership has been assigned. Government is by far the most important mechanism for nonmarket social cooperation, given that it owns natural assets on our behalf. But the natural liability of carbon is singular in being global rather than national. It is completely pointless for an individual country to assume the liabilities for the carbon generated on its territory unless other countries do so as well. What is needed is global cooperation.

The Wages of Sin and Opportunistic Morality

Discussion about carbon is dominated by the idea of a global deal on "cap-and-trade." Rights to the emission of carbon, up to a safe global limit, would be assigned to countries, firms, and people, and these rights could then be traded. Those who wish to emit more carbon than their "entitlement" would buy the rights from others.

Such discussion is rife with moralizing and opportunism, both of which were on display at Copenhagen. The moralizing is a bizarre echo of medieval Christian theology in which sins are divided into those of omission and those of commission. The Bible tells us resoundingly that "the wages of sin is death." The medieval church took this to the literal extent of putting a price on each sin and then selling forgiveness, transactions known as "indulgences." The popes used indulgences as the chief means of financing the construction of St. Peter's in Rome. The modern environmental variant of this moral framework is the sin of *emission*. The wages of sin have become global warming. Instead of frying in hell, we will fry on earth. And the modern variant of an indulgence is a carbon-trading right. The rich can keep committing sins of emission so long as they buy a carbon offset. Governments may well be attracted to carbon trading for the same reason as the medieval papacy: they are short of money and selling the trading rights would generate a lot of it. Just as the medieval popes could finance St. Peter's, so President Obama could finance the budget deficit.

The opportunism stems from the lobbying done to grab these rights. Indeed, the economic theory of rent-seeking provides an alarming insight: the resources devoted to lobbying may escalate to equal the value of the rights that can be acquired. The value of carbon-trading rights is potentially vast. The typical estimate of the value of a ton of carbon is around $40 and for the ceiling on emissions around 18 billion tons. Hence, the potential value of carbon-trading rights is a staggering $720 billion per year—an annual Toxic Assets Recovery Program.

Since neither natural assets nor natural liabilities have natural owners, anyone can join the scramble for carbon rights using whatever reasonable-sounding arguments they can find. For example, a country might argue that it should have rights to emit carbon based on the carbon it was emitting when the cap was imposed. Or the right to emit as much carbon as some other country. Or because it is poor. Or because it did not emit any of the carbon that caused the problem.

Rent-seeking over carbon rights can occur both nationally and internationally. At the national level it is already apparent in the U.S.

Congress. Potentially, the assignment of carbon rights could make the huge rent-seeking machine that is the American agricultural lobby look like a side-show. Internationally, the scope for scams may well be even larger. Firms that want to continue emitting carbon simply need to purchase a piece of paper certifying that some firm somewhere elsewhere is emitting correspondingly less carbon than it otherwise would have done. The carbon-emitting firm has no interest in the integrity of this claim. As for the carbon-reducing firm, according to the current Clean Development Mechanism, that firm does not actually have to reduce its carbon emissions. It merely has to reduce them relative to what they otherwise would have been. It merely has to show convincingly that it would have emitted a lot of carbon. Because the CDM operates piecemeal, unrelated to any overall framework, a country can be paid again and again for avoiding specific emissions while actually increasing its total emissions without limit. The sale of indulgences through the CDM creates incentives not to reduce carbon emissions but to threaten to increase them by as much as possible.

In effect, the Clean Development Mechanism has the same flaw as the granting of valuable fishing rights to fishermen for nothing. Recall that while fish are abundant fishermen can catch whatever they like, and the value of a fish merely reflects the cost of catching it. As the maximum sustainable harvest is reached the value of a fish rises; it becomes a valuable natural asset with a scarcity rent. As I've argued, fishermen should not automatically be entitled to that scarcity rent on what has become a natural asset. We can apply the same reasoning to carbon emitted by coal-burning power stations. When global emissions of carbon were below their safe level there were no costs to carbon; anyone was free to run a power station. Once everyone wants to run a power station there are costs to carbon. The rights to inflict those costs do not follow from activity during the period when there were no costs. Once carbon has become socially costly, the power stations that previously belched it out without consequence should now meet those costs. Similarly, new power stations cannot claim a right to belch simply based on the fact that before carbon was socially costly other power stations did so for free. If by threatening to start belching I thereby acquire the right to be compensated for not doing so, the global bill for compensation can rise without limit.

The moralizing and opportunism have confused the subject of carbon emissions. The debate is being driven by a desperate quest to avoid owning the liabilities while claiming as many rights as possible. This has detracted from the more fundamental issue of how a natural liability should be managed. Forget about who has done what to whom, or who is to blame for the current stock of carbon, or who should pay whom to compensate. Instead, we should focus on what it means now that we have discovered carbon to be a liability.

Essentially, calling carbon a liability implies that activities which generate it are producing something harmful. However, they are also producing something useful and usually that something will be much more valuable than the damage done by carbon. Usually, but not always. Take coal mining. In the hierarchy of fuels coal is quite costly to exploit relative to its value in fuel, which is why coal-mining areas in many developed countries are in trouble. Extracting coal is not sufficiently profitable to pay competitive wages. Not only is coal not that valuable, it emits carbon. How much depends upon the type of coal; some types are better than others. Until we became aware of global warming, in low-wage countries coal was worth mining. Now, burning coal produces not just heat but carbon. That coal should now be left in the ground rather than mined; it has become socially worthless. That may change if and when new carbon-capture technology gets developed, but that technology will itself likely be costly.

What Would a Low-carbon World Look Like?

The world needs to function in such a way as to emit no more than a safe level of carbon. What would such a world look like? Economics offers some useful insights, at least in terms of telling us the principles that should govern an efficient world economy. Efficiency is often best understood by its opposite—inefficiency. It would, for example, be inefficient were one activity allowed to belch out carbon while producing very little of value, while another activity, one which produced highly valued output, was not allowed to generate any carbon at all. Another example of inefficiency would be were an activity—say, a chemical plant—moved to a country where it functioned less efficiently but where carbon regulation was more generous. There is a very compelling reason why we should care about efficiency: global warming is bad news. Dealing with it is going to be expensive, and not dealing with it is going to be even more expensive. We should therefore deal with it in the most efficient way possible. All inefficient responses are needlessly more costly than efficient responses and can easily become ruinously expensive.

The big idea in economics is price. Price denotes value. For most goods the market price really is the same thing as its social value: the price approximates both to the cost of producing the good and to the value consumers attach to it. Economists are such enthusiasts for the market because for most things it represents by far the best mechanism for squeezing out as much social value as possible. However, economists also recognize that some goods generate social costs or benefits that are not priced in the market. At present, carbon is such a good. You can belch out carbon for free but it is going to incur costs to other people. Extending the concept of price, economists have come up with the notion that where social value diverges from the market price we can estimate a notional or "shadow" price which does reflect true cost. Given that we know that carbon is socially harmful, its price should be negative. People should have to pay to produce it.

Now for the useful insight: the world will respond to the problem of carbon emissions efficiently if, and only if, the shadow price of carbon is the same for everyone everywhere. This is where the aforementioned $40 comes in. Economists estimate that the shadow price of carbon at which people would in aggregate emit no more than the safe level is around $40 per ton. There is a wide margin of potential error around this estimate. We do not know how much carbon is safe to emit, and we do not know how people would respond if faced with a price for emissions. But for the moment, let's stick with that estimate.

Let us return to the question of what the world would look like were everyone faced with a $40-per-ton price. Most activities would not be affected, for they emit very little carbon relative to the value of the output that they generate. For example, most service activities, which dominate modern economies, would scarcely notice the difference. The same would be the case for most light manufacturing; it uses very little carbon-generated energy relative to output.

Heavy industry, agriculture, and energy-producers are quite different. Some heavy industries emit huge amounts of carbon; unless they changed technologies their costs would rise sharply. As their costs rose consumers would respond by shifting patterns of consumption away from the products. Agriculture may look "natural," but it is a very carbon-intensive activity. It isn't just about the farting cows. When stubble is burned off a field, it spews out carbon;

when land is tilled it also spews out carbon. Agriculture will need to adapt.

Energy-production is, of course, the most carbon-emitting activity. However there are huge variations. The worst offender is coal. In effect, the shadow price of coal is now the market price minus the cost of the carbon it emits. In many cases coal is now worthless and mines need to close. The continued expansion of coal mining is an instance of social plunder analogous to the looting of Africa's natural assets: private gain at the expense of others. Coal mining is a tough life. My own surname is no coincidence: my ancestors were colliers—coal miners. It is a cruel accident of nature that those who braved the dangers of mining coal should inadvertently have become social predators, but that is the reality. The world must curtail carbon emissions and coal is the most egregious carbon-generating activity on the planet.

At the other end of the spectrum from coal is nuclear power, which is entirely carbon-free and which perfectly divides the romantic environmentalists from the pragmatic environmentalists. The romantics are sometimes perversely gleeful about global warming, for it means that capitalist industrialization will get its come-uppance. However, the news that salvation lies in nuclear power is anathema, encapsulating everything they most hate about industrial capitalism. With its high science and large scale, nuclear power is about as far removed from "being at one with nature" as it is possible to get. The romantics prefer wind power, tidal power, and solar power, all of which are readily intelligible to ordinary citizens; nuclear power harnesses forces of nature only intelligible to a scientific elite. Unfortunately, however, wind, wave, and sun power are not yet scalable in the way that nuclear power is scalable. By far the most carbon-efficient advanced economy is France, which, following the oil shock of 1974, decided to achieve energy security by investing in nuclear power. France was able to do this because whereas elsewhere the political left was hostile to nuclear energy, in France it was nationalistic and so supported the idea of independence from imported oil. Wind, wave, and solar power may eventually become scalable (provided enough money is put into research), but for the moment pragmatists such as Stewart Brand, one of the pioneers of the environmental movement, have accepted that nuclear power is an essential part of the battle to contain global warming. They are in tune with the spirit of this book, which is that decisions over the management of natural assets and liabilities are too important to be guided by romanticism.

Faced with a shadow price for carbon of around $40 per ton, the world will gradually respond efficiently to global warming. In an adjusted world, coal mining will have radically contracted, along with some heavy industries, and agriculture will have adapted. How about ordinary consumers? Overall, our energy consumption may not need to change that much. For example, in France, where electricity comes predominantly from nuclear power, it is cheaper than in England where it comes predominantly from gas and oil. So, in a carbon-compatible world we will not need to switch off all the lights. But some sources of energy will need to change.

The most dramatic change will involve the fuel for vehicles. Oil, after all, is liquid carbon. The world simply cannot take a billion or more vehicles running on carbon. Fortunately, there are alternatives: either batteries that have been charged from noncarbon sources of energy or ethanol. The issue is simply one of technology. Recently, I was invited to Brussels to give a talk. Somewhat bizarrely, the venue was an auto museum, and as I roamed among the magnificent vintage relics of former technology I realized how massive had been the technical advances of the last century. My own truly basic car would have been considered a sensational advance had it been exhibited at an auto show even fifty years ago. Can the auto industry evolve away from carbon-based fuel? Of course it can. Underlying the choice of technology is the matter of incentives. In the absence of incentives auto manufacturers are inadvertently part of the plunder machine. They are making a living by selling a product that is bought because the social costs that it inflicts are not borne by the purchaser. Europe has already faced its consumers with incentives to economize on carbon-based fuel, and so the adjustment should be relatively painless. The new technologies are unlikely to cost significantly more than the current price of fuel. In contrast, American consumers have grown accustomed to paying a price for gas that does not reflect its social cost. While this is bad news for American consumers, they should keep in mind that a socially realistic price for energy would not destroy the quality of life.

Some industries will need to adjust more than others, some consumers more than others, and some countries more than others. Which ones and how much will follow from thinking through the most efficient response for industries and consumers, and then mapping those responses onto the countries where industries and consumers will be located. Unfortunately, the international political negotiations on global warming are approaching the issue back-to-front. The big international conferences—Kyoto and Copenhagen—give rise to haggling between national governments over who should pay what to whom. Instead, we need to start from the principle of efficient response—a commonly agreed-upon world shadow price of carbon, and work from that.

Emissions Will Shift as Industries Relocate

The efficient response to a common shadow price for carbon will not imply that everyone in the world emits the same amount of carbon. One of the key premises of economic geography is that it is efficient for an industry to cluster. Different industries will efficiently cluster in different places. The best place may be the one in which the costs of transport are minimized, balancing the costs of bringing in raw materials against those of delivering the product to its markets. Different industries will have radically different carbon emissions. As a result, some countries may be the most efficient home of carbon-emitting clusters of industry, while others should house low-carbon activities. This tells us something that may be politically quite inconvenient but is economically quite important: a globally efficient response to global warming will not involve each country's emitting the same amount of carbon per head of population. It will, however, involve a particular industry's emitting the same amount of carbon per unit of output—wherever it is located.

At present, most of the big carbon-emitting industries are clustered in the rich countries. But industries move. The principle of efficient response to global warming tells us that no industry should have an incentive to relocate simply due to its carbon emissions. Nonetheless there are many other legitimate reasons why industries shift. In recent decades industry has been growing more rapidly in the emerging economies of Asia than in the high-income countries, so that the proportions have been shifting. But from now on this shift will not only be proportionate, it will be absolute.

The United Nations Industrial Development Organization asked me to put together a team to produce an Industrial Development Report. As we delved into the data one of our simplest findings most surprised me. Industrial output in the high-income countries has been steadily decelerating, decade by decade; in the developing world, especially Asia, it has been accelerating. Simply extrapolating these contrary trends led us to the conclusion that 2008 was likely to be the peak year for industrial output in the high-income countries; after 2008 it would start an absolute decline. By the time we published the Report, in March 2009, industrial output in the high-income world was indeed already in serious decline due to the global economic crisis. But commentators missed the larger context of the shift of industry from the developed to the developing world. We predicted that the fall in industrial output in the high-income economies will turn out not to be temporary. When global industrial output recovers, much of the extra production will be located in developing countries. We have entered the phase of absolute industrial decline in the rich world. The coming decades will echo to the long, receding roar of its contraction. Other than those involved in the most complex processes, industry will be clustered predominantly in middle-income countries, with light manufacturing clustered in low-income countries. As a result, carbon emissions will automatically shift to the developing world. The high-income world will find itself concentrating on services, which are low-emission activities.

A Common Harm Needs a Common Tax

So how can the world get to the most efficient solution to global warming? International cap-and-trade would indeed achieve a common global price for carbon and this, or its equivalent, is indeed essential for efficiency. However, international cap-and-trade is not the only way that a common price could be achieved. Indeed, it might politically be an extremely difficult way of achieving a common global price. The most straightforward way would be for each government to impose a carbon tax at the same rate—for example, $40 per ton. We will worry later about who should end up paying for global warming; for the present I want to stick to the issue of how we get an efficient response. Were every government to impose a carbon tax of $40, industries and consumers worldwide would coordinate around this price. No activity would have an incentive to relocate to dodge the social cost of its emissions. Nor would some consumers be spewing out carbon wastefully while others were behaving responsibly.

Some economists prefer to regulate the quantity of carbon emissions directly rather than starting with price. This is the argument of Nicholas Stern, whose work on climate change has rightly been hugely influential. His argument is based on an underlying theory which, though complicated in detail, makes in essence a very simple distinction between stipulating quantities and stipulating prices. Sometimes we know the social cost and do not know what quantities will be produced at this cost, and sometimes we know the quantity that would be socially desirable but do not know the price that would bring about this quantity. Where we know the social cost we should set a price—in this case a carbon tax—and where we know the social quantity we should regulate the quantity—carbon permits—and let the market find the price of these permits.

However, the theory is most appropriate for one-off situations. The Rolling Stones give a farewell concert. There are only so many thousand seats to be sold, and nobody knows what the demand will be. The efficient solution is to auction the tickets rather than to set a price in advance. In regards to carbon emissions, we know that they must be reduced drastically, but other than that we are in the dark until technology evolves and behavior changes. The relevant quantities of carbon emissions are in the distant future. If $40 turns out to be an unnecessarily high price it can be lowered, and vice versa. Since adjustments are inevitably going to be gradual, setting a price which evolves would have much the same effect as setting a quantity which evolves.

Before we dismiss the idea of a commonly agreed shadow price for carbon as politically unrealistic, we should consider that there is one huge political advantage to settling on a price compared with trying to agree to a quantity. Agreement on a global quantity requires agreement on who has what quantities. This is the foundation for the approach of international cap-and-trade, whereby each country would be given an emission right and be able to sell it to others. Because natural liabilities have no natural owners, there is no bedrock principle to which we can appeal. In contrast, agreeing to a common shadow price for carbon does not require assigning ownership of a natural liability. It has an underlying appeal in that inefficiency and unfairness coincide. It would be inefficient if the chemical industry in one country faced a lower price of carbon emissions than the same industry in another country, and it would also be unfair, because workers in the chemical industry in the first country would lose their jobs to workers in the other country. The workers who benefited would be guilty of plunder, enriching themselves by running up a natural liability that had to be paid for by others.

Supposing that each country agreed to work with a common shadow price of $40 for carbon, what would this imply at the national level? One possibility is that each government would simply introduce a carbon tax of $40. This would be the most straightforward approach. It does not imply a heavier overall tax burden. There is no reason for a government to use a carbon tax to raise its total revenue take; rather, a carbon tax might replace other taxes. It is manifestly better to tax a social bad, such as carbon, than to tax something which is socially beneficial, such as work. So a tax of carbon could be offset by a reduction in the taxation of income, or some other tax regarded as particularly irksome. However, agreeing on $40 would not necessarily require a carbon tax. The task of achieving compliance by firms and consumers can be done by whatever means a society prefers. In some cases direct regulation may be much easier than taxation. Indeed, the same activity can be subject to a carbon tax in some countries and a regulation in others, as long as the two are equivalent. It would be surprisingly easy to tell whether they were equivalent, for the industry would emit the same amount of carbon per unit of output in each country. As long as this principle was accepted, the mixture of tax and regulation could safely be left as a choice for each society. For example, the cap-and-trade approach could be used for trading within a nation much more readily than between them, since nations already have the political architecture to assign rights among citizens. Or governments could simply regulate. The state of California, for example, has led the way in regulating the auto industry into producing low-emission vehicles. This is helpful because it provides the industry with clear targets. In Europe there has also been a mixture of tax, cap-and-trade, and regulation; for example, light bulbs are now required to be energy-efficient.

The Geo-politics of Common Taxation

Armed with some sense of what an efficient response would look like, now consider the international politics involved in getting there. Who turns out to be the good guys and who the bad guys may surprise you.

What is needed is global cooperation, and we know how hard that is to achieve. The key problem is what is termed "free-riding." Whether we fry from global warming depends not upon one individual, but upon everybody. Since my decision whether to reduce my emissions does not determine your decision, the sensible thing for me to do is nothing. I should simply hope that everyone else reduces their carbon emissions. If they do I am safe regardless of what I do, and if they don't I will fry regardless of what I do. Either way, I might as well avoid the cost of reducing my carbon emissions.

Government is the key solution to the free-rider problem. Within a country, a government can force a change of behavior through taxes and regulations. But carbon emissions are a global problem and so the free-rider problem kicks in at the level of bargaining between governments. There is plenty of scope for free-riding among the 194 countries of the world. Whether or not Guinea Bissau agrees to curb its carbon emissions will make no difference to global carbon emissions, and no difference to whether other governments agree to curb their carbon emissions.

However, not every government can credibly regard itself as a free-rider. Start with the two really big countries, the United States and China, sometimes now referred to as the G2. Each knows that unless it agrees to a carbon deal there can be no global deal. Fortunately for the rest of the world, both the United States and China have a strong interest in avoiding global warming. If the planet heats up, Florida will sink beneath the waves and the Himalayas will melt. As Florida sinks and waterfront properties become uninsurable, there will be mounting pressure from wealthy residents. The presidential election of 2000 was decided by a handful of voters in Florida, choosing between one candidate who regarded fighting global warming as the top priority and another who regarded it as a non-issue. I predict that by 2050 any presidential candidate who says that global warming is a non-issue will resoundingly lose in Florida. Should the Himalayas melt the consequences for China would be similarly politically explosive. Both governments therefore have an interest in cooperating. We now know that by the end of his second term, while publicly still belittling the issue of climate change, President Bush entered into secret climate negotiations with China. I was not surprised: governments have to face reality. The same willingness to work together was manifest at Copenhagen: much to the chagrin of the Europeans, the final text was put together by the G2.

So the United States and China are unlikely to be the problem. Rather, they jointly face the problem of getting the rest of the world to stop free-riding. Europe is unlikely to be problematic. To date Europe has led the world on the issue of carbon emissions and it will not want to fall behind China and the United States. Further, much of the climate change agenda can be handled at the level of the European Union rather than in each of the 27 member countries. In aggregate the EU is a very large economy, far too large to regard itself as having the potential to free-ride. Similarly, Japan is a large economy and has a long record of behaving as a responsible global citizen.

So far we have the G4—the United States, China, the EU, and Japan—with incentives to behave responsibly. In view of its enormous size I will add India to this group of the responsible nations; it, too, is simply too large to free-ride. To date Indian governments have been a little reluctant to step up to the responsibility implied by their country's size, but they will likely come to terms with its global role and responsibilities. In any event, beyond the G5, it gets harder because each of the other countries in the world could reasonably adopt a strategy of free-riding, and if they all did so the consequences would be dire. Worse, these countries have an incentive not simply to free-ride, but actively to undermine the efforts of others. Analogous to tax havens, it is to their individual advantage to provide carbon havens in which emissions are unrestricted. If this happens, the carbon-emitting industries would simply shift to these locations. The G5 would have reduced their emissions, but not global emissions. And as this happened the political will to incur the costs of reducing emissions might easily evaporate even among the G5. The world would fry because of the plunder by the G163.

What I have sketched is a weakest link problem: any solution is only as effective as the behavior of the least cooperative country. The problem for the G5 is therefore to provide some combination of carrots and sticks that addresses the free-rider problem in the G163. The carrots and sticks do not have to be the same everywhere. Obviously, the G163 would prefer carrots to sticks. However, there is a good reason sticks are likely to offer a better approach. The problem with the carrot approach is that the negotiating range is vast. The G5 might start by offering to cover the full cost of reducing carbon emissions. This is the lowest figure that would give the G163 an incentive not to free-ride. But the G163 would know that the potential benefit of their cooperation is far in excess of this: the potential benefit is the cost of global warming to the G5. In other words, the G163 have an incentive to try to exploit the situation. In fact, the full extent of the problem goes beyond that. Given the weakest-link property of the problem, there is a strong incentive for each individual country to be the last country to agree. In a weakest-link problem, the most recalcitrant country can potentially hold out, waiting to be given an amount almost equal to the costs of global warming. With only carrots it will be difficult to reach any agreement.

In contrast to carrots, sticks have the helpful property of inducing more countries to cooperate, because the longer a country free-rides the higher the penalties. No country wants to be the only noncompliant place on earth and face alone the cost of these sticks.

The easiest countries for the G5 to persuade to comply are the bottom billion, because for them the costs of compliance are modest and because they are mostly substantial recipients of aid. There is indeed the potential danger that the bottom billion will be bullied into better behavior than can be induced elsewhere. In effect, the G5 has the scope to condition the receipt of aid on the adoption of an effective national strategy for low-carbon growth. By "low-carbon growth" I mean a pattern of growth consistent with a shadow price of carbon of $40. For example, industries would either face a national carbon tax at this rate or be required to comply with regulations that set carbon emission standards at levels equivalent to those of other countries. For such a deal to work, the aid potentially foregone by noncompliance would need to be more valuable than the alternative of noncompliance, real or imagined. Moreover, given the history of aid, donor offers and threats would not be fully credible. If, as is likely, the extra aid for compliance is partially discounted due to limited credibility, the aid offer will need to be all the larger. So aid to the bottom billion needs to be linked as closely as possible to a commitment to low-carbon growth, and be made as generous as possible. The sheer scale of the problem means that this is not a matter of creating yet another special aid fund for climate change, but, rather, of integrating policies for low-carbon growth into the entirety of future aid programs which will themselves need to be enhanced. Virtually all economic activities emit carbon, and so the switch to low-carbon growth has to be viewed comprehensively. Aid will need to be intelligent and it will need to be generous—neither characteristic having been notably prominent in aid to date. (For the moment I will park discussion of the ethics of using aid to force compliance with global carbon standards and turn to the other countries that might potentially free-ride.)

The low-income countries are not the core of the free-rider problem. Between them they do not emit much carbon, and even if they offered global industry a haven from action against carbon other aspects of their business climate might deter relocation. The key problem group is the emerging market countries, which collectively emit a lot of carbon. They offer credible havens for the evasion of global carbon policy, and do not receive significant amounts of aid. What stick could be used against such countries?

Regrettably, the only credible leverage is likely to be trade restrictions. I say "regrettably" because trade restrictions are a stick to which governments are all too tempted to resort: they provide the attractive political illusion that the restrictions benefit "us" by penalizing foreigners. Over the years the international community has learned to limit recourse to trade restrictions by building an international institution to police them. This is the key role of the World Trade Organization. The WTO demonstrated its worth with the onset of the global economic crisis in 2008. In contrast to the depression of the 1930s, governments did not impose the beggar-thy-neighbor policy of trade restrictions as a means of fighting the recession. However, as the U.S. Congress has recently realized, it might be possible to impose trade restrictions upon countries that do not comply with a global carbon policy without breaching the rules of the World Trade Organization. Although the actual level of retaliatory tariffs that might be justified under WTO rules looks to be very modest, were I the Minister of Trade for a middle-income country the thought that the G5 would have a legitimate excuse to impose trade restrictions against me would chill me to the bone. Once unleashed, trade restrictions against a small middle-income country can become devastating, for example by frightening off investment. The threat of trade restrictions would be an effective stick for most middle-income countries.

Between them the carrots and sticks of aid and trade cover most of the G163 though not all. The remaining countries are those not poor enough to receive aid, and who only export primary commodities not affected by trade restrictions. Essentially, they come down to the energy exporters, such as Russia and the Middle East.

These are the countries that have most to lose from a successful global reduction in carbon emissions: *they are the exporters of carbon*. The $40-per-ton social cost of carbon makes their stocks of carbon fuel far less valuable. That they are the ultimate victims of climate change is probably the most reasonable ethical outcome. As we know, natural assets such as oil have no natural owners. It is merely a social convention (and acceptance of the realities of political power) that the stock of natural assets beneath the ground is deemed to be owned by whichever society lives above them. The societies sitting on top of valuable deposits of carbon fuel have by chance enjoyed uncreated wealth; now that those uncreated assets are less valuable they have no cause for complaint.

Think what the price of oil is likely to be in 2060. According to the Hotelling Rule, the price of oil should by then be astronomic, its price increased cumulatively by the world rate of interest. But that is not going to happen. Instead, advances in technology induced by the need to reduce carbon emissions are going to reduce the demand for oil. Investments in nuclear power, solar energy, and bio-fuels may between them have lowered the price of energy, and carbon-based energy will in any case sell at a discount to clean energy. The exporters of carbon-based energy may have no incentive to comply with a global curb on the use of carbon, but while their economies remain based on the export of carbon fuel they cannot do much to undermine action by the rest of the world. They will simply be the victims of a decline in global demand for their exports. As they face this decline in demand, they will have a strong incentive to diversify their economies toward other industries. To the extent that they succeed they become more exposed to the stick of trade restrictions. Just as they get into a position to exploit being the weakest link, inducing industries to relocate to their territories, the threat of trade restrictions would begin to be effective.

Victims and Villains

What I have sketched is, I believe, the real geo-politics of global warming. It stands in stark contrast to the current global discourse, which led inexorably to the failure of the Copenhagen summit. In the prevailing discourse the United States and China are the twin villains because they are the key emitters of carbon, and the developing countries are the victims because they will suffer the most severe consequences of global warming without having been responsible for causing it.

The moral discourse on global warming starts from the attribution of blame, or, to return to the caricature of medieval Christian theology, of guilt. Industrial capitalism is guilty of polluting the world with carbon and must now pay for its sin. This morality tale is music to the ears of those in the rich world who hate industrial capitalism: an alliance of the anti-industrial values of the aristocracy, exemplified by Prince Charles, and the anti-capitalist values of Marxists. It is also seductive to the marginalized societies of the bottom billion, which aspire to industrial capitalism but have not achieved it. They sense the opportunity to refresh the guilt-ridden colonialist hangover: the West is responsible for their poverty. Global warming gives colonial guilt a new lease on life. Victimhood is back in business. Approaches to climate change are encumbered by such ethical baggage, much of it unhelpful.

Here is another thought experiment to cut through the thicket. Suppose scientists discovered that the reason why we in the North die before we reach the age of 150 is that cassava, a crop grown by poor peasant farmers in Africa, emitted ions which corroded the air in northern latitudes. Does this discovery give us all a claim for compensation from African farmers? The answer, obviously, is that it does not. Since the farmers did not know, they incur no liability. Now push this one step further. Once the science is accepted, what should happen? Clearly, African peasants should cease to grow cassava, but who should bear the cost? Should Africans simply recognize that killing us is an unacceptable price to pay for growing their favorite crop, or should we in the North compensate them for not killing us? Having decided who should pick up the liability for those deathly cassava ions, apply the same principle to global warming. The baggage encumbering climate change—sin and guilt—is not intrinsic to the structure of the problem, but imported from other agendas.

A further thought experiment. Suppose that the entire world had industrialized at the same time as the West. Carbon emissions would have built up beyond dangerous levels before scientific knowledge advanced sufficiently to understand it properly. Our understanding of climate change would still only really have become convincing around the millennium, by which time it would have been too late. Alternatively, if none of the world had industrialized, we would not now have the problem of global warming, but nor would we have the ability to deliver prosperity. The painful but reasonable conclusion is that it was fortuitous that only part of the world industrialized. This gave science the time to understand global warming in time for us to take preemptive action. The corollary of such a skewed pattern of global industrialization is that some societies have remained impoverished.

The case for helping the bottom billion, a case I believe is overwhelming, is that they are needy because they have been unlucky enough not to have had the opportunities open to the rest of us. The basis for helping them is not that they are victims of our industrial greed. Had no part of the world industrialized there would be no path to prosperity. Had every part of the world industrialized we would now be frying. As it is, we have learned that it will be entirely feasible for the world to industrialize and prosper as long as we all make the relatively modest adjustments involved in low-carbon growth. Nobody need feel guilty about past carbon emissions. Nobody is entitled to feel victimized. However, the lucky parts of the world should behave generously toward those that have been unlucky.

That the poorest parts of the world should be the ones most severely affected by climate change is a further stroke of ill-luck and so a further powerful reason why the rest of the world should help to bear the burden. The rich world should be prepared to meet the costs that the bottom billion incur in adapting to the climate change that, even with global mitigation, is inevitable. We should compensate societies that are poor for these further slings and arrows of outrageous fortune. We should be prepared to meet, and indeed exceed, the costs that they will incur in miti-gating their future emissions. Otherwise the free-rider problem will overwhelm us all. Nonetheless, the foundation for generosity should be compassion and enlightened self-interest rather than compensation for liability. On present plans for an enhanced Clean Development Mechanism, China and the other emerging market economies are best placed to threaten the increased emis-sions that the CDM pays to avoid. Yet ethically, their claims on the rest of mankind are very much weaker than those of the bot-tom billion.

A final thought experiment. Suppose that the carbon-emitting industries do end up clustered in middle-income countries, with the high-income countries engaged in low-emission services. I sus-pect that within a few decades this will prove the most globally efficient allocation of economic activity. Should the middle-income countries then pay the high-income countries for the "right" to emit carbon? Such an outcome would evidently be ridiculous, yet that is where the rights-based arguments might lead us.

The central issue in global warming is not who should compensate whom for past sins of emission. It is that the world should adjust as efficiently as possible—which, remember, means at the least possible cost—to a low-carbon future. The issue of who compensates whom is completely independent of this problem and, as with all natural assets and liabilities, has no clear guiding principles by which ownership of carbon liabilities can be assigned. Indeed, there is a famous economic theorem by the Nobel Laureate Ronald Coase which makes precisely this point. The efficient outcome is independent of how the property rights are assigned. Because international cap-and-trade creates national property rights for emissions, it provokes an intense international struggle over how these rights should be assigned. The alternative that I have suggested is that governments should agree to a common set of taxes-cum-regulation that curb global emissions to safe levels and do not induce activities to relocate to evade facing social costs.

Even the long-term international cap-and-trade proposal that each person on earth should be given the same emission rights for carbon is liable to be gamed. In practice, the revenues from these carbon rights would accrue to governments, not to individuals. A government could game such an allocation formula in various ways. The least damaging would be to inflate the country's population figures. In case you think this is fanciful, precisely this happened in Nigeria and for a very similar reason. Nigeria is a federation. Once oil was discovered, it was agreed to distribute part of the revenues to the state governments based on their populations. A census was conducted, but its actual implementation in each state was the responsibility of the state government. As the results of the census were added up, it was found that the population had exploded: each state government had encouraged its census workers to inflate the figures. So, if carbon rights are to be based on population, we will soon no longer be able to trust the census results, at least for some countries.

The most damaging way in which a government could game its carbon rights would be to destroy its economy. If people are desperately poor they emit little carbon. President Mugabe of Zimbabwe has recently demonstrated how effectively an economy can be destroyed. Zimbabwe now emits little carbon, so the government would be entitled to the global average emission rights paid to it on behalf of the Zimbabwean population. The carbon checks would roll in to President Mugabe as the difference between average global emissions and the pitifully low emissions of Zimbabweans. In effect, governments would be rewarded for creating poverty.

Everywhere in the world, firms and people should be faced by common incentives, or their regulatory equivalent, to curb carbon emissions. Once we accept this principle, we can then apply our earlier discussion of the ownership of natural assets. The most sensible arrangement is for governments to own the rights to control carbon emissions on behalf of citizens. As industries relocated between countries, according to underlying legitimate economic incentives, the amount of carbon emitted would also shift between countries. So if governments imposed carbon taxes as their instrument for enforcing low-carbon growth, the revenues from carbon taxes would also gradually shift between countries. This is not really any different from other natural assets. Each country's endowment of natural assets changes both as a result of what is discovered and as global technology makes some commodities more valuable and others less. The rents on nature shift around; so will the rents on carbon. This is all the more reason not to try to freeze national entitlements by some once-and-for-all grand assignment. After all, the need to curb carbon emissions is going to be with us for a long time.

Back to the Future

Global warming does raise a major distributional issue, one between
the present and the future. Because carbon remains in the atmosphere for decades, it is a long-term liability. Like the plunder of
natural assets, excessive emissions of carbon plunder the future:
a private gain today comes at the cost of a larger loss for others
tomorrow. How should we think of our responsibilities to future
generations? We are back to the Utilitarian ethics of saintly ants
pitted against an environmental ethics, one in which each generation has custodial responsibilities not to infringe the rights of other
generations.

According to the Utilitarian calculus the only thing that weakens the claim of the future is that it will be richer than we are. The
rich are assumed to enjoy an extra dollar less than the poor and
so, on the greatest-happiness principle, helping the rich future at
the expense of the poorer present is inefficient. Other than that, a
person in the distant future should receive exactly the same consideration as a person alive today. Therefore, if, by sacrificing a trillion
dollars today by curbing carbon emissions we can avoid losses of
say five trillion dollars to people living in the twenty-second century, this is a good deal—unless, that is, those future people are so
much richer than we are that the last five trillion dollars to them
confers less utility than the one trillion dollars to us. In all prob-
ability the distant future will be very much richer than we are, and
thus according to the Utilitarian calculus that future prosperity is
a major impediment to the case for current action. Indeed, some
recent work on climate change within the Utilitarian framework
has argued that without action climate change will be so severe that
the future will be poorer than we are. If the future is going to be
poorer, the Utilitarian calculus is far more convenient for advocates

of carbon reduction: a transfer to the future becomes more rather than less valuable in terms of utility.

Is the issue different viewed from the ethics of custody? Carbon is a renewable natural liability entirely analogous to renewable natural assets. We have rights of custody, which for renewable assets is a sustainable rate of harvest. For a liability, the equivalent is a sustainable rate of carbon emissions at which the global climate is not affected. As with any natural asset, our custodial responsibility does not amount to an absolute requirement to preserve. We are not ethically obliged to keep the climate constant. But, if we decide to emit more carbon than the sustainable rate, we are obliged to compensate the future by bequeathing assets which match the extra natural liabilities that we are imposing. We are not entitled to plunder the future without compensation. What, in the case of carbon, does full compensation mean? Responsible custody means taking decisions about which future generations should reasonably say, "Yes, that's fine by us."

To see how the ethics of custody make a difference, we need to return to the implications of the notion that future generations might be much richer than we are. For the Utilitarian calculus this weakens the claim of the future upon us. But one effect of their being much richer is that they will value things differently. Our descendants will likely have man-made goods in abundance, and therefore are likely to value the scarce natural world more highly than we do. They will place a high value on a decent climate.

We don't have to peer into the future to see this at work today: visit Haiti. Haiti is a hot, mountainous and very unequal island. The income hierarchy maps unerringly into the height at which people live. Poor people are crowded at the bottom of the hills, rich people live at the top of the hills, and the middle classes live in the middle.

In a hot world, cool will be a luxury. This has an unfortunate corollary for us: if our descendants are going to be a lot richer than we are, they are going to value a decent climate far more than we do. So, if we decide to let rip with carbon emissions rather than incur the costs of curbing them, we are morally obliged to compensate. We can compensate our descendants for an inheritance of a hot climate by giving them other goods, except unfortunately, they will already have such goods in abundance, and we will therefore need to give them an awful lot of them before they finally say, "That's fine by us."

Why Carbon Is Like Lobsters

The ethics of carbon emissions is, in fact, a little like the ethics of lobsters. Lobsters are a renewable natural asset and a luxury. According to the ethics of custody we are entitled to eat the sustainable harvest of lobsters without compensating the future. However, it would be ruinously expensive to eat more than that. We would need to compensate the future for having eaten them and the future, being rich, will value lobsters even more highly than we do. According to the ethics of custody, the richer future citizens are going to be, the greater the need for us to curb our carbon emissions.

This is precisely the opposite implication of the Utilitarian calculus. The richer our descendants, the less we should preserve for them. I should add that sophisticated analysts such as Nicholas Stern readily accept the idea that values change with income. Nor is he wedded to Utilitarianism, recognizing that other ethical perspectives are equally legitimate. Nonetheless, it remains the case that disputes among economists over the costs and benefits of curbing carbon emissions are almost exclusively fought according to the terms of the Utilitarian calculus.

The ethics of custody, which I would argue most closely matches the perspective of many environmentalists, tells us quite unequivocally that we should not warm the planet through excess carbon emissions. If we do, we are obliged to compensate the future for carbon liabilities by handing down an equivalent amount of man-made assets. Equivalence means that the future would not feel aggrieved with what we have done, and yet, because the future will be awash in man-made assets, such equivalence may demand compensation beyond our means.

Curbing carbon is most likely to be the cheapest option that is consistent with our ethical obligations. Utilitarian ethics reaches the same conclusion, but by a different route that demands that we should be saintly ants, valuing people in the distant future as much as ourselves. Recognizing that people are not remotely like this, Utilitarian economists despair of popular opinion and count on governments to ignore their citizens. Such a dismissal of popular opinion is neither legitimate nor necessary. Although most people are not saintly ants, nor are they the greedy individualists of economic models. They recognize that their rights over nature are not as absolute as their rights over the man-made world. Popular opinion need not lead to plunder; it can be the foundation for natural order. But we cannot afford to be naive about popular opinion: ethics is not enough. People must also understand the natural world. If they misunderstand it, things can go horribly wrong.

Nature Misunderstood

Nature Misunderstood

CHAPTER 10

Nature and Hunger

SO FAR THIS BOOK HAS BEEN A PLEA that nature can be entrusted to the values of ordinary citizens. But my confidence is conditional upon people taking the trouble to be reasonably well informed about the scientific and economic issues involved. The natural assets of the bottom billion will continue to be plundered unless a critical mass of ordinary citizens realizes the importance of getting the key decisions right: the chain of decisions set out in part II. Carbon will continue to accumulate as a natural liability unless an equivalent critical mass is built, country by country. Informed societies are feasible, but they are not inevitable. Our relationship to nature brings into play powerful emotions and ordinary people can sometimes be misled into beliefs that may seem comforting but ultimately are destructive.

Between 2005 and 2008 the world price of basic foods jumped by over 80 percent. In the slums of the poorest countries the children of the poor went hungry; had the price spike persisted they would have suffered stunting. This adverse shock had its origins in muddled popular beliefs about nature that have become increasingly common in the rich societies. In this chapter I am going to show how three such misconceptions exposed some of the world's poorest children to hunger.

In the poorest societies the rise in food prices was a major political event. To the typical household in these societies food is the equivalent of energy in America: if the price rockets people expect their government to do something. There were riots in some thirty countries; in Haiti they brought down the government. The increase in prices proved to be temporary; the global economic crisis was an effective though catastrophic remedy. But we cannot rely upon economic crises to come to the rescue. We need to understand why it happened and what can be done to prevent its recurrence.

The immediate policy responses to the food crisis were dysfunctional even by the dismal standards of most international responses. They included beggar-thy-neighbor, pressure for yet larger farm subsidies, and a retreat into romanticism. Neighbors were beggared by the imposition of export restrictions by the governments of food-exporting countries. This had the immaculately dysfunctional consequences of further elevating world prices while at the same time reducing the incentive for the key producers to invest. Unsurprisingly, the subsidy-hunters seized their opportunity: Michel Barnier, the French agricultural minister, urged the European Commission to reverse the incipient reforms of the Common Agricultural Policy. The romantics who had long found scientific commercial agriculture distasteful portrayed the food crisis as demonstrating its very failure. They advocated the return to organic small-scale farming. Yet a return to antiquated technologies simply cannot feed a prospective population of nine billion.

Cheap food is going to be increasingly important because the poor will increasingly be unable to grow their own. As populations grow and the Southern climate deteriorates due to global warming, the South will necessarily urbanize. The future populations will live not on quaint little farms but in the slums of coastal megacities. They will not grow their food but buy it, and they will buy it at world prices. The only way it will be affordable is if it is produced in abundance. The technical challenges to producing reliably cheap food are surmountable but political opposition will be intense.

Feeding the world will involve three politically difficult steps. Contrary to the romantics, we need more commercial agriculture, not less. The Brazilian model of large high-productivity farms could readily be followed in areas where land is underused. For example, half of the land area of Zambia—a vast expanse of around 150,000 square miles—is arable yet uncultivated. Again, contrary to the romantics, the world needs more science. The European and consequential African ban on genetically modified crops is slowing the pace of productivity in the face of accelerating demand and Americans need to face down the romanticism that bio-fuels will secure energy supplies. Beneath the rhetoric of self-sufficiency lurks the lobby for subsidies. I propose a political deal: mutual de-escalation of folly. In return for Europe's lifting its self-damaging ban on GM (genetic modification), America could suspend its self-destructive subsidies on bio-fuel.

Why Did Food Prices Rise?

Typically, in an attempt to find a solution to a problem people look to its causes, or yet more fatuously, to its *root* cause. However, there need be no logical connection between the cause of a problem and appropriate or even feasible solutions. Such is the case with the food crisis. The root cause of the sudden spike in prices was the spectacular economic growth of Asia. Asia is half the world and its people are still poor and so devote much of their budgets to food. As Asian incomes rise, so, too, does demand for food. Not only are Asians eating more, they are eating better: carbohydrates are being replaced by protein. It takes six kilos of grain to produce one kilo of beef, and so the switch to protein is raising grain demand. The two key parameters in demand are income elasticity and price elasticity. As a rule of thumb, the income elasticity of demand for food is low: if income rises by a fifth demand for food will rise by around a tenth. The price elasticity of demand for food is only around one-tenth; people simply have to eat. This implies that were the supply of food fixed, to choke off an income-induced increase in demand of 10 percent the price would need to double. As this example illustrates, quite modest increases in global income will drive prices up alarmingly unless matched by increases in supply.

The rise in Asian incomes, though spectacular, was not abrupt. The price spike of 2005–8 was reinforced by supply shocks, such as the prolonged drought in Australia. Supply shocks will become more common because the rising levels of carbon in the atmosphere increase climatic volatility. Against a backdrop of relentlessly rising demand, supply will fluctuate more sharply.

Who Gets Hurt by Expensive Food?

By no means all poor people are adversely affected by expensive food. Those who are farmers are largely self-sufficient, and though they may buy and sell food, the rural markets on which they trade are often not integrated into global markets and thus impervious to the surge in prices. Where poor farmers are integrated in global markets, they are likely to be beneficiaries. However, the good news needs to be qualified. Although most poor farmers will profit most of the time, they will lose precisely when they are hardest hit: during famine. The World Food Programme is designed to act as the supplier-of-last-resort to famine-stricken localities. Yet its fixed budget shrinks in terms of buying power when food prices surge. Paradoxically, the world's insurance program against localized famine is itself acutely vulnerable to global food shortages. High global food prices are good news for farmers but only in good times.

The unambiguous losers from high food prices are the urban poor. Most of the developing world's large cities are ports and, barring government controls, the price of their food is set on the global market. Crowded in slums, the urban poor cannot grow their food; they have no choice but to buy it. By a cruel implication of the laws of necessity, the poor spend a far larger proportion of their budget on food, typically around a half; high-income groups in contrast spend only around a tenth. Hungry slum dwellers are unlikely to accept their fate quietly. For centuries sudden hunger in slums has provoked violence. This is the classic political base for demagoguery and the food crises would provoke its ugly resurgence.

But we have still not arrived at the end of the food chain. Among the urban poor those most likely to go without food are children. If young children remain malnourished for more than two years the consequence is stunting. We now know that stunting is not merely a physical condition; stunted people are not just shorter than they would have been, their mental potential is impaired. Stunting is irreversible: it lasts a lifetime, and indeed, some studies find that it echoes down the generations. Although high food prices are yesterday's news, a few successive years of them will create tomorrow's nightmare. And tomorrow would last a long time.

Global food prices *must* be kept down. The question is how. Short of repeated global economic crises there is nothing to be done about the increase in the demand for food. The solution must be to increase world food supply. Of course, world food supply has been increasing for decades; it has more than kept up with population growth. But we now need it to be accelerated. Global food production must increase more rapidly than it has in recent decades. Because prices need to be kept down during the demand rebound that will be part of the postcrisis recovery, we need to see a substantial expansion of the food supply soon. However, the "root cause" of the food crisis is a faster rate of increase in demand, and although a step increase in the short-term supply is urgently needed, it will soon be overtaken by continued growth in demand. Hence, we also need to increase the rate of growth of food production over the medium- and long-term.

Our own policy makers have the power to increase supply by changing regulations; by encouraging organizational changes; and by encouraging innovations in technology. However, each of these is currently blocked by a giant of popular romanticism: all three giants must be confronted and slain.

Giants of Romanticism 1: Peasants-in-Aspic

The first giant that must be slain is the middle-class love affair with peasant agriculture. With the near-total urbanization of the middle classes in both America and Europe, rural simplicity has increasingly acquired an allure. The simple farm life is prized as organic in both its literal and its metaphorical sense: Prince Charles is one of its leading apostles. In its literal sense, organic agricultural production is now a premium product, a luxury brand: indeed, Prince Charles has one such brand. In its metaphorical sense, it represents the antithesis of the large, hierarchical, impersonal, and pressured organizations in which so many in the middle classes now work. Prince Charles has built a model village, in traditional architectural style. Peasants, like pandas, are to be preserved.

Distressingly, peasants, like pandas, show surprisingly little inclination to reproduce themselves. Given the chance, smallholder farmers in poorer countries seek local wage jobs and their offspring head to the cities. This is because at low-income levels rural bliss is precarious, isolated, and tedious. The life forces millions of ordinary people into the role of entrepreneur, for which most are ill-suited. In successful economies a majority of people invariably opt for wage employment, so that they can leave to others the worry and grind of running a business; entrepreneurship is a minority pursuit. Reluctant peasants are right: the mode of production is ill-suited to modern agricultural production where scale is helpful. Technology is constantly evolving; investment is lumpy; consumer food fashions are fast-changing and met by integrated marketing chains; and regulatory standards are rising toward the Holy Grail of traceability of produce back to source. All these modern developments are better suited to large, commercial organizations. Of course, they could be ignored were agriculture to return to subsistence cultivation— the romantic vision taken to its *reductio ad absurdum*. Far from being the answer to global poverty, organic self-sufficiency is a luxury lifestyle.

Local self-sufficiency in rich countries is being encouraged through the concept of "food miles"—the ideal being the shortest route between production and consumption. But there is no virtue in minimizing the transportation of food. Indeed, from the perspective of carbon emissions it usually makes more sense to grow food in the most conducive climates, wherever they are, and transport it. The image of vegetables being flown around conjures up carbon profligacy, but the key carbon emissions are in cultivation not transportation. While *food miles* do not reduce carbon, they do reduce incomes in the bottom billion: horticulture for export creates scarce rural jobs.

Nor will organic self-sufficiency produce the food the world needs. It might be appropriate for burnt-out investment bankers, but it won't feed hungry families. Large organizations are better suited to cope with innovation, investment, marketing chains and regulation. Yet for years the development agencies have been basing their agricultural strategies upon encouraging smallholder farm production. This approach is all the more striking given history. For example, the standard account of how English economic development started in the eighteenth century is that the enclosures movement enabled by legislative changes permitted the development of large farms, which in turn sharply raised productivity. Although current research qualifies this conventional account, reducing the estimates of productivity gains to the 10–20 percent range, to ignore commercial agriculture as a force for rural development and enhanced food supply is surely ideological.

Large organizations can internalize those effects that in smallholder agriculture are localized externalities, and thus not adequately absorbed. In the European agricultural revolution innovations indeed occurred on small farms as well as on large ones, and today many small farmers, especially those that are better off and better-educated, are keen to innovate. Nonetheless, agricultural innovation is highly sensitive to local conditions, especially in Africa, where soils are complex and variable. Innovators create benefits for the locality and, to the extent that these benefits are not fully captured by the innovators, improvement will be too slow. One solution is to have an extensive network of publicly funded research stations with advisors who reach out to small farmers. However this model has largely broken down in Africa, an instance of more widespread malfunctioning of the public sector. In eighteenth-century Britain, the innovations in smallholder agriculture were often led by networks among the gentry, who corresponded with each other on the consequences of experiments. But such processes are far from automatic; they did not occur in continental Europe. Commercial agriculture makes it easier.

Over time African peasant agriculture has fallen further and further behind and based on current trends the region's food imports are projected to double over the next quarter-century. Indeed, during the recent phase of high prices the United Nations Food and Agriculture Organization (FAO) worried that smallholder farmers would *reduce* their production because they could not finance the increased cost of fertilizers. While there are partial solutions through subsidies and credit schemes, large-scale commercial agriculture simply does not face the problem. If output prices—the cost of food—rise by more than input prices—the cost of making the food—production will expand not contract.

Successful agriculture is, indeed, staring us in the face. The Brazilian model of large, technologically sophisticated agro-companies has demonstrated how food can be mass-produced. To give one example, the time between harvesting one crop and planting the next—the downtime for land—has been reduced to an astounding thirty minutes. The Brazilian model has provoked horror because one of its effects has been the depletion of the rain forest and the displacement of indigenous populations. Parts of Brazil had the conditions in which unregulated commercialism would indeed inevitably lead to these outcomes. But much of the poor world is not like that: the land is not primal forest, it is just badly farmed. Sometimes the Brazilian model can bring innovation to smallholder farming, such as in the "out-cropping" or "contract farming" model, by which small farmers supply a central business with specified qualities to schedule. Depending upon the details of crop production, this may be more efficient than wage employment.

The leading international expert on African agriculture is Hans Binswanger, now a professor emeritus of economics at the University of St. Gallen in Switzerland. In 2009 the FAO invited us both to Rome to debate the issue of large commercial farming versus smallholder farming. Our common ground turned out to be that the future of African agriculture is unquestionably *commercial*; the issue on which we disagree is that of *scale*. Hans believes that family farms, albeit consolidated into larger units than at present, will prove to be the most viable, whereas I think that much larger farm units might be more efficient.

We each came up with an analogy to make our point. Hans's analogy was that farms are like restaurants. Yes there are large cafeteria-style eateries, but family-run restaurants predominate because the advantages of having motivated workers offset the disadvantage of not being able to purchase food in bulk. Customers know this and vote with their feet. My analogy was that farming is like retailing. Africa's peasant farmers are the equivalent of the vendors you find on every street corner in African cities. Street vending is an activity of desperation, one that will be wiped out by supermarkets, which benefit from technology, finance, and logistics in ways that street vendors cannot hope to match.

Large farms are the supermarkets of agriculture. Scale has become more important because technology, finance and logistics have all changed. The decades of productivity stagnation in African peasant agriculture has opened up a huge gap between family farms and commercial agriculture. As cultivation has become more sophisticated, the inputs (like fertilizer) have become more expensive. Whereas industry has been able to economize on inventories of inputs by just-in-time production systems, agriculture has intrinsically long lags between planting and harvesting and so is now more finance-intensive than most other activities. Logistics loom much larger because agricultural output is no longer mainly for local consumption. It is global. Technology, finance, and logistics are all inherently replete in economies of scale.

Hans and I did not resolve our differences, but I suspect that we are not that far apart. Many family farms will indeed be viable: they will commercialize and take over the holdings of neighbors whose children leave for the cities. However, such farms will be a far cry from the peasant of the romantic idyll—producing for subsistence rather than the market, and using traditional, organic techniques uncontaminated by science. These family farms will co-exist with much larger commercial farms, with whom they will both compete and cooperate. Co-existence will in part be competitive but it can also be cooperative. Large farms can buy the raw output of surrounding small farms for processing and marketing. They can also provide the financing for inputs.

There are many areas of the world that have land which could be used far more productively were it properly managed by large companies. Indeed, large companies—some of them Brazilian—are queuing up to manage them. Yet over the past forty years African governments have adopted the opposite approach. Large-scale commercial agriculture has been scaled back. At the heart of the matter is a reluctance to let land rights be marketable, and the likely source of this reluctance is the lack of economic dynamism in Africa's cities. In the absence of "investing in investing," cities have not generated sufficient decent jobs. In consequence, land is still the all-important asset; there has been little investment in others. As a natural asset, land, unlike those assets produced by investment, has no natural owner. It is a gift of God and its ownership conferred by a political act. In more successful economies, land has become a minor asset and so the rights of ownership, though initially assigned politically, are simply extensions of the rights on other assets, and thus can be acquired commercially.

A further consequence of a lack of urban dynamism is that jobs are scarce, and so the prospect of mass landlessness evokes political fears: the poor are safer on the land where they are less able to cause trouble. President Mugabe traded on these fears in denuding Zimbabwe of its commercial agriculture. The right response to the illegitimacy of colonial land acquisition was to nationalize land and lease it back, rather than to destroy the productive value of commercial agriculture. In the process of returning his country to subsistence cultivation President Mugabe has brought a once-fertile country to conditions of mass hunger, with famine averted only by emigration and food aid.

How large should large farming be? The global food crisis panicked the governments of some food-scarce countries into a scramble for African land. The political panic button was not just the sharp rise in global food prices, but the export bans that many of the food-exporting governments promptly imposed. Those bans signalled that market relationships could not be relied upon to feed people; in fact they were liable to be overridden just when they were most needed. South Korea struck a deal with the government of Madagascar to acquire a huge area of the country on a 99-year lease. As news leaked out the deal destabilized the government and led to a successful coup d'état. Other such deals are apparently underway. Saudi Arabia is purchasing land in Ethiopia, and the United Arab Emirates is purchasing land in Sudan. While the United Nations has denounced such deals as a new wave of colonialism, the analogy doesn't always apply. In 2009 an African nation, Libya, purchased 100,000 hectares of Europe in the Ukraine.

Although I favor commercial agriculture, these new land deals are not properly commercial. The motivation behind them is primarily to bypass the global market, not to participate in it. The deals are too opaque, too large, and too long. As a result, they take us back to the deficiencies of trying to sell prospecting rights to a single company. If land is to be farmed in large commercial units, those units should be auctioned among an adequate number of bidders. If, as is likely, the first investors face radical uncertainty as to what the returns will be, only a few such blocks should be sold during the first wave. The price bid will inevitably be heavily discounted to take that uncertainty into account. But as the pioneers learn how best to cultivate the new lands, this knowledge is likely to raise the value of the remaining land which should therefore be sold later. Nor should any single commercial farm be allowed to become so large that it becomes the dominant employer in a whole region. An important role of government is to prevent the abuses that follow from private monopolies. The largest food-importing country not to have joined the scramble for African land has been Japan. Instead, the Japanese government has pressed the G20 to restore order in world food markets by banning the bypass deals. The trigger point for the land grabs was the export bans on food. That is precisely what should be regulated, and the appropriate institution to do that is the World Trade Organization. The equivalent behavior on imports, bans and quantitative restrictions, is now prescribed by WTO rules; the same principles should be extended to exporting.

Even if such land grabs are contained, global agribusiness is still too concentrated, and a sudden switch to an unregulated land market within the poorest countries would probably have ugly consequences. But allowing commercial organizations gradually to replace some smallholder agriculture would increase the global food supply in the medium term.

Giants of Romanticism 2: The GM Ban

The second romantic giant is the European fear of scientific agriculture, which has been manipulated by the agricultural lobby into yet another form of protectionism: the ban on genetically modi-fied (GM) crops. GM crops were introduced globally in 1996 and already account for around 10 percent of the world's crop area, some 300 million acres. But due to the ban virtually none of this is in Europe or Africa. Robert Paarlberg brilliantly anatomizes the politics of the ban in his recent book *Starved for Science*. By ill-luck, in 1996 Europe was in the grip of a food heath crisis: Bovine spongiform encephalopathy, or BSE. The BSE tragedy was caused by the sway the farming interests had over the British public agency of health regulation: they were literally in the same government ministry. Government officials and ministers initially tried to reas-sure consumers that British beef was safe. Famously, the Minister of Agriculture made his young daughter eat a hamburger in front of television cameras. No sooner had she done so than the minister was forced to eat his words: around the country people began to die in the most ghastly way imaginable—by their brains rotting away. (As of October 2009, the number of deaths from Creutzfeldt-Jakob disease—the human variant of BSE—stood at 165 in Britain, and 44 elsewhere.)

Across Europe pro-protectionism groups seized the opportu-nity and called for the ban of British beef. BSE has nothing to do with genetically modified food, but it set the precedent. Geneti-cally modified food, so disastrously named as to be a car crash waiting to happen, became portrayed as Frankenfoods: a scientific experiment on consumers. To cap it off, GM came from research by American corporations like Monsanto and so provoked predictable and deep-seated hostility from the European left. Thus were laid the political foundations for a winning coalition—protectionism and anti-Americanism—amplified by the paranoia of health-conscious consumers who no longer trusted government assurances.

In the years since the ban was introduced, the political coalition has expanded its base, even though the scientific case for lifting it has become progressively more robust. The latest high-profile supporter of the ban is Prince Charles, who represents an important constituency of opinion distinct from the founding trio. His views on GM reflect his broader opposition to scientific-commercial agriculture. His vision is, of course, appealing to those of us hemmed into modern industrial life. But watching the aristocracy farm in imitation of the ways of a bygone rural society, another image crept into my mind: that of Marie Antoinette playing at being a dairy maid in Versailles. It soothes the soul, but it does not feed the stomach.

The GM ban, which immediately followed BSE, has had three adverse effects. Most obviously it retards productivity. Prior to 1996, when the ban was introduced, European grain yields tracked those in the United States, whereas since they have fallen behind by around 1–2 percent per year. European grain production could be increased by around 15 percent were the ban lifted. Europe is a major cereal producer, so this is a large loss. And because Europe is out of the market for GM technology, the pace of research has slowed. Research takes a very long time to come to fruition and its core benefit—the permanent reduction in food prices—cannot fully be captured through patents. Hence, there is a strong case for supplementing private research with public money. European governments should be funding this research, which instead is entirely reliant upon the private sector. Private money, in turn, depends upon the prospect of sales, so the European ban has not only blocked public research it has stifled private research.

The worst consequence of the European ban is that it panicked African governments into banning genetic modification (the only exception being South Africa). They feared that otherwise they would permanently be shut out of selling to European markets.

Because Africa banned GM, there was no market for discoveries pertinent to the crops that Africa grows, and therefore no research. In turn, this led to the critique that GM is irrelevant for Africa.

Africa simply cannot afford this self-denial. It needs all the help it can possibly get from genetic modification. For the past four decades African agricultural productivity per acre has stagnated. Increased production has been dependent on the expansion of the area under cultivation. But with population still growing rapidly, this option is running out. On the horizon is climatic deterioration due to global warming. The climate forecasts are that most of Africa will get hotter, that the semi-arid parts will get drier, and that rainfall variability will increase, implying more droughts. Indeed, it seems likely that in southern Africa, the staple food, maize, will become unviable. Whereas for other regions the challenge of climate change is primarily about mitigating carbon emissions, in Africa it is primarily about agricultural adaptation.

It is conventional to say that Africa needs a Green Revolution. The reality is that the Green Revolution has been fueled by chemical fertilizers, and even when fertilizer was cheap Africa did not adopt it. With the rise in fertilizer costs—as a by-product of high energy prices—any African Green Revolution will perforce not be chemical. To counter the effects of a rising population and a deteriorating climate, Africa needs a biological revolution. This is what GM offers, but only if sufficient money is put into research. There has as yet been no work on the crops of key importance to the region, such as cassava and yams. GM research is still on the first generation: single-gene transfer, in which a particular gene that gives one crop an advantage is identified, isolated, and added to another crop. But even this infancy stage offers the credible prospect of vital gains. Maize can be made more drought-resistant, buying Africa time in the struggle against climatic deterioration. Grain can be made dramatically more resistant to fungi, reducing the need for chemicals and cutting storage losses. For example, stem borers—insects that do just that—cause storage losses in the range 15–40 percent of the maize crop; a new GM variety is resistant.

Like commercialization, genetic modification will not be the magic fix for African agriculture; there is no such fix. But without it, the task of helping African food production keep abreast of its population looks daunting. While Africa's coastal cities can be fed from global supplies, the vast African interior cannot be fed in this way (other than in emergencies). Lifting the ban on GM, both in Africa and Europe, could hold down global food prices in the long term. Recently, African governments have begun to rethink the ban. Burkina Faso, Malawi, and most recently Kenya have lifted it.

Giants of Romanticism 3: Grow Your Own Fuel

The final romantic giant is the American fantasy that it can escape dependence upon Arab oil by growing its own fuel. There is a good case for growing fuel, but not from grain: the conversion into ethanol uses almost as much energy as it produces. This basic fact has not stopped the grain lobby from gauging out grotesquely inefficient subsidies. Around a third of American grain has been diverted into energy, a switch that demonstrates both the superb responsiveness of the market to price signals, and the shameless power of subsidy-hunting lobbies. If the U.S. wants to run off agro-fuel instead of oil Brazilian sugar cane is the answer; it is a far more efficient source of energy than grain. The smoking gun of the protectionism at work here is that the American government has actually *restricted* imports of Brazilian ethanol to protect American production. The sane goal of reducing dependence on Arab oil has been sacrificed to the self-serving goal of pumping yet more tax dollars into American agriculture.

The huge diversion of grain for ethanol has had an impact on world prices. Quite how large that impact is has been hotly debated. The Bush administration claimed initially that it had raised prices by only 3 percent, but a study by the World Bank suggests much higher. Were the subsidy lifted there would probably be a swift impact on prices: the supply of grain for food would increase.

The Politics of Change: Deals and Alliances

The three giant-killing policies—permitting the expansion of large commercial farms, lifting the GM ban, and lifting the subsidies on ethanol—fit together both economically and politically. In economic terms they fit together both in their implications for the timing of increased production and through linkages in production. Lifting the ethanol subsidies would bring short-term relief. The expansion of commercial farms could, over the next decade, raise world output by a few percentage points. And both measures would buy the time needed for GM to deliver its potential. The lag between starting research and its mass application is around fifteen years. The expansion of commercial farming in Africa would encourage GM research in Africa-suited crops, and these innovations would find a ready market less sensitive to political interference. It is not by chance that the only African country in which GM was not banned is South Africa, where the organization of agriculture is predominantly commercial.

In political terms the three policies are also complementary. Home-grown energy, the banishment of Frankenfoods, and preserving the peasant way of life are each classic populist programs. They sound appealing but they do harm. They must be countered by messages of equal potency.

One such message is the scope for international reciprocity. Although Americans are attracted to home-grown fuel, they are rightly infuriated by the European ban on GM. They see the ban for what it is: anti-American protectionism. Conversely, Europeans cling to the illusory comfort of the ban on high-tech crops, but are rightly infuriated by the American subsidies on ethanol. They see the subsidies for what they are: a selfish desire to maintain American energy profligacy that condemns the world to global warming. Over the past half-century America and Europe have learned how to cooperate. The General Agreement on Tariffs and Trade, inaugurated in 1947, virtually eliminated tariffs on manufactures over the ensuing decades. NATO was an accumulating partnership in security. The OECD was an accumulating partnership in economic governance (the collective ban on bribery to win contracts is an instance of the cooperation it has achieved). Compared to the challenges of finding agreement in these areas, a deal calling for the mutual de-escalation of environmental follies scarcely seems daunting. America should agree to scrap the ethanol subsidies in return for Europe's lifting the ban on GM. Each side can find this deal infuriating and yet attractive, since each side should find it politically feasible to persuade its constituencies that the result will be better than the status quo.

Overcoming the hostility toward commercial and scientific agriculture will be more demanding. It will require some soul-searching among environmentalists as to their true priorities. Many feel acute concern for the poorest countries. In both America and Europe millions of decent citizens are appalled by global hunger; each time news of a famine reaches the popular media the response is overwhelming. The combination of concern about poverty and concern about the environment can be a potent force for good. The ethics of the custody of natural assets provides a secure foundation for policy toward the natural world.

Nonetheless, the alliance between environmentalists and economists to harness nature for development cannot elide the hard choices. We will not beat hunger by returning to prescientific, precommercial agriculture. Environmentalists will need to agonize over their priorities. Some may decide that the vision articulated by Prince Charles is the more compelling: a historic lifestyle must be preserved regardless of its consequences. Personally, I find that vision highly attractive. Once I become a burnt-out professor it may be the lifestyle I choose. But faced with the prospect of stunted children I balked: for me the vital matter for public policy is to increase food supplies. I believe that many people, once they do the painful thinking, will share my priorities. Commercial agriculture may be irredeemably unromantic, but if it is part of the route to full stomachs then it should be harnessed to that purpose.

American environmentalists will also need to do some painful rethinking. The people most attracted to energy self-sufficiency through ethanol are potentially the constituency that can save America from its ruinous energy policies. The cruel truth is that the United States indeed needs to reduce its dependence upon imported oil, but that growing bio-fuel is not the answer. America is quite simply too profligate in its energy use. Europeans, themselves pretty profligate, use only half the energy per capita and yet sustain a high-income lifestyle. The American tax system needs to be shifted from burdening work to discouraging energy consumption.

A key quality of good politicians is guiding citizens away from the kind of populism that, unless countered, will block the policies needed to address the food crisis. For those living in the United States and Europe high food prices will be an inconvenience, not dire enough to force us to overcome the three giant myths on which populism rests. Our political leaders need to deliver this message and forge new alliances. If they don't children will go hungry and their futures will be impaired. The painful task of dismantling our romantic illusions cannot be avoided.

Natural Order

CHAPTER 11

Restoring Natural Order

FOR EARLY MAN, little of the natural world was valuable. The few natural things that were useful were abundant, and therefore undemanding. Now, thanks to technology, far more of the natural world is useful, but it must satisfy the demands of over six billion people. Abundance has been superseded by scarcity, not because the natural world has diminished but because we now know how to exploit it. The result, in the absence of effective rules, and in its various manifestations, is plunder.

Some of the things we might think of as natural are already adequately protected. The fish in a fish farm, the trees planted in a private forest: these are managed within a framework of incentives that is compatible with social interests. But there are two major holes in the protective web, and too much is falling through them. One hole is created by bad governance, and the other by the limitations of good governance. In other words, one is created locally, by specific governments in the countries of the bottom billion and their management of natural assets, and the other is global and involves management of those assets beyond national boundaries.

The nonrenewable natural assets in the territories of the bottom billion are seldom harnessed for the development of their societies. As a result, future generations may inherit a depleted natural world with little to show for it. The once-only chance of using assets to lift these societies out of poverty through harnessing them will have been missed. The governments of many of the poorest countries are insufficiently held to account by their citizens for the good management of the natural assets under their control.

The international renewable natural assets, such as the fish of the high seas, are liable to be plundered to extinction, while the natural liabilities, such as carbon, are liable to accumulate. The fish will have been eaten, and the carbon emitted, predominantly by the citizens of the rich countries. Throughout this book I have been guided by the haunting question of what future generations will think of us. Even good government stops at national frontiers that these natural assets and liabilities transcend. How can these two holes be closed?

Harnessing Natural Assets in the Poorest Countries

I will start with the seemingly intractable problem of unaccountable governance in the bottom billion. In part II I set out the chain of decisions that need to go right in order for a low-income society to become prosperous through its natural assets. I also set out the evidence that the chain usually breaks because the incentives for plunder are too strong, and the opportunities for it are too abundant. Development through natural assets is subject to the weakest link problem. If anywhere along that long chain of decisions the forces of plunder triumph, the entire process fails. Not only do the decisions have to be got right, they have to stick. It takes at least a generation for the investment financed by the extraction of natural assets to bring about social transformation. For that whole generation the society is vulnerable to plunder.

How can poor societies harness the potential of their natural assets? The international community has no power over the governments of these societies, which however bad they are, cannot be forced to do what they do not want to do when it comes to management of the natural assets. The government of Angola does not need our money; it gets plenty from its oil and diamonds. The only chance that such societies will manage their opportunities equitably is if enough of their citizens form a critical mass of informed opinion. Along that whole chain the right decision will be taken again and again when it is subject to social pressure. Such pressure need not work through the discipline of elections in order to be effective. Ministers and senior officials are drawn from a social network whose attitudes they are likely to respect. At a minimum, that social network needs to understand the opportunity constituted by natural assets, and the role of each decision in realizing it. The individual incentive to plunder can be countered when each decision is viewed as a potential weak link, and the enormous benefits to getting it right seen clearly.

While the international community cannot tell the governments of resource-rich countries what to do, it can make it much easier for societies to build that critical mass of informed opinion. The place to start is in making public the potential revenues from resource extraction. The small NGO Global Witness ran a campaign, Publish What You Pay, which pioneered the idea of a voluntary international standard for reporting revenues. That campaign has now evolved into an international organization, the

Extractive Industries Transparency Initiative (EITI). The organization is run by a consortium of stakeholders and sets voluntary standards which governments can adopt. Although EITI is a recent organization, already more than thirty governments have signed up. Its success depends upon a world-wide alliance between civil society and political leadership, but the weight was on the former. According to the official records, former British Prime Minister Tony Blair launched the Initiative at a breakfast event in Johannesburg. Actually, he did no such thing. Worried that it might not attract sufficient support, he used the breakfast to talk about something else. The Initiative got launched because government officials forgot to alert the press office to the change. The press release announcing the Initiative went out by mistake. If an initiative with such an inauspicious start can nevertheless succeed, it cannot be too difficult to make a difference.

While the EITI is the right place to start, it would clearly be the wrong place to stop. Integrity in reporting the flow of revenues is necessary but far from sufficient to ensure that natural assets have transformational power. In *The Bottom Billion* I floated the suggestion that what was needed was a charter for natural resources which set out clearly the entire decision chain for everyone—ordinary citizens, technocrats, and ministers—to understand.

One of the major problems in getting international coordination is that in regards to cross-cutting issues such as this, no single organization has the convening power. The Fiscal Affairs Department of the International Monetary Fund put out a lengthy document on the management of natural assets, so I discussed the idea with them. Ruefully, they admitted that their difficulties of coordination had started even within their own organization. Other departments of the Fund had not exactly responded with alacrity, and as for global coordination—well, forget it. Yet around the world, academics, civil society, and government officials were pushing for the idea of a charter, particularly with the commodity boom coming to a peak. But there was just no organization to do it. An informal group of people started to think about what such a charter should contain. We began to flesh out the content. The group cohered into a team under the auspices of Michael Spence who, through his work on leading the Growth Commission, came to share the view that mismanaging natural assets was a major missed opportunity. With lawyers (both academic and practicing), tax specialists, and political scientists, we hoped to bring together the minimum skills needed to address the problem.

We started to consult with the many pertinent organizations: the resource-extraction companies, the NGOs, the international organizations, governments, and academics. In the process we made a remarkable discovery. These organizations and individuals were more willing to cooperate with us than they were to cooperate with each other. Our very insignificance was a source of strength. We began to wonder whether, as with the emergence of the EITI, in current international conditions coordination might be easier to achieve from below than from above.

Building agreement among a group of academics, practitioners, and organizations is inevitably a gradual process, involving workshops, writing retreats, and presentations. Much of this could be done without the need for money, but as the Charter grew and started to attract attention, individual philanthropists, NGOs, and governments all started to get interested. Recognizing the power that comes from the independence of the insignificant, they offered funding without expecting ownership. Three political giants from resource-rich countries agreed to constitute the board that would take responsibility for the Charter. Ernesto Zedillo, the former president of Mexico who is now a professor at Yale, agreed to chair the group. He was joined by Chukwuma Soludo, who during his tenure as Governor of the Central Bank of Nigeria won the international accolade of Central Bank Governor of the Year. The third member of the trio was Yegor Gaidar, the Prime Minister who had led the economic reforms in Russia. With President Zedillo, Governor Soludo, and Premier Gaidar constituting the Board, and Mike Spence leading the supporting technical group, the Charter makes up in natural authority what it lacks in institutionalized power.

With its core content agreed, and a credible leadership, the Charter was ready to reach that critical mass of citizens. The conventional approach is through international events. The Charter was launched at parallel events in Dakar, at the annual meeting of the African Development Bank, and in Oslo. Both the Bank and the Norwegian government were concerned that never again should a commodity boom go to waste. But such events cannot directly reach citizens. In earlier decades the task of reaching beyond a tiny group would have been virtually hopeless. Now the Internet makes it easy. The entire Charter is posted for all to see at NaturalResourceCharter.org. It is currently organized in three levels: one that provides a two-minute overview of its twelve Precepts; one that provides straightforward expositions of each precept for citizens and journalists; and one that is designed to offer more of the detail that a practitioner might need for implementation, including guidance on how to learn more than the Charter itself can provide. The Internet has enormously enhanced the ability of ordinary citizens to communicate with each other collectively.

If you doubt the power that this new form of communication has opened up, view Clay Shirky's 2009 talk on TED@State: I was lucky enough to be in the audience (I was giving the next talk).

As he demonstrated, the collective power of citizens is not confined to the rich, democratic societies; it is a reality even in the authoritarian states. Clay's example is China, where technology enabled citizens to hold corrupt officials to account for the shoddy construction of schools that collapsed during earthquakes. If that can happen in China it can happen in most of the societies of the bottom billion. Once some mistaken decision catches attention, and citizens realize that their best opportunity to catch up with the rest of mankind is being wasted, they have the power for collective action as never before. Citizen power is the cornerstone of the Charter. Such power need not be the enemy of government; government needs an informed society to protect it from the pressures of populism.

Potentially, the Charter is an international convention in-the-making, with the difference that it is being generated from the bottom up, rather than from inter-government cooperation. There are supposedly only six degrees of separation between any two people on earth. For the first time in history we have a technology that can span those degrees of separation. Just as the readership of *The Bottom Billion* helped to create the Charter, I hope that the readership of *The Plundered Planet* will collectively learn from Clay Shirky and help to spread the ideas that make a difference.

The Responsibility Not to Be Complicit in Plunder

If the Charter evolves into an international convention, what might be its long-term potential? Clearly, the primary purpose of the Charter is to help the citizens of resource-rich countries harness their natural assets for prosperity. Some societies will succeed in managing the entire decision chain; others will continue to fail.

For the latter, the ethical implications of failure need to be clear to everyone, such that any person or organization participating in the exploitation of natural assets would be complicit in plunder. It would no longer be a valid defense for a resource-extraction company to say that it had held to the terms of a legal agreement with a recognized government. The company would have the responsibility of participating in a process of due diligence, establishing that the government was acting responsibly when it signed the agreement. After all, the powers of government officials over natural assets are not unlimited. A company that aided and abetted crude plunder or personal theft would be complicit.

But, of course, part of the argument of this book has been that a government can also be guilty of a more sophisticated form of plunder—by failing to save and invest sufficiently. The Charter could potentially evolve into an international convention which enabled companies to judge whether a government was meeting its responsibilities to the future. Companies that exploit natural assets in a country in which the government was not meeting its responsibilities would, again, be complicit with plunder.

At this point I can feel the collective shudder running down the spine of the resource-extraction companies based in the rich countries. I can also hear their response. "If we are barred from operating in these environments," they might reasonably argue, "we will simply hand the business over to companies beyond the range of accountability." But the truth is that companies, like individuals, face a choice as to whether to be complicit. The defense, "Had I had not facilitated plunder, someone else would have done so," cuts no ice in a court of law, and it should leave us unmoved. There is also a more worldly-wise response, which I will introduce via a discussion of how to fill that other hole in the regulation of the natural world.

Achieving International Coordination

The countries of the bottom billion might often have dysfunctional governments but at least they have governments. While their citizens will have their work cut out holding their governments to account for the responsible custody of nationally owned natural assets, citizens elsewhere will need to hold their governments to account for the responsible custody of global natural assets and liabilities.

That second hole is created by the absence of government above the level of the nation-state. Addressing it means counting upon inter-government cooperation and unfortunately, in the last decade, the ability of governments to cooperate has dramatically declined. The first and best evidence of this decline comes not from the front-page news stories involving Afghanistan or Iran, but from a story reported on the business pages: the collapse of the Doha Round of trade negotiations. Governments have been participating in these negotiations, or rounds, organized by the World Trade Organization, for fifty years. Their point is to lower trade barriers. Each round has been roughly similar storyline: given the potential for large mutual gains, negotiators haggle until they reach a deal which, though not perfect for anyone, represents an improvement. The Doha Round (named for the city in Qatar where it started), which has been going on for far longer than any other round, is the first complete failure. Somehow, somewhere, negotiating governments have lost the storyline.

The global food crisis of 2008 offers further evidence of the decline in inter-government cooperation. It rapidly exploded into a trade war: most of the major grain-exporting developing countries imposed export bans, which drove up global prices in the short term and reduced investment in grain production in the longer term.

A final example of the decline in inter-government cooperation was the initial responses within Europe to the global financial and economic crises. During the onset of the crisis, individual governments offered deposit guarantees to their banks, inadvertently inducing depositors to shift their accounts from those banks whose governments had not offered guarantees. A decade previously Europe had been better able to cooperate, agreeing to the Stability Pact and launching the Euro.

This decline has collided with the emergence of problems which can only be addressed effectively by common international responses. Both carbon and fish are such issues. Since reductions in carbon emissions and in the fish catch by anyone are equally valuable, each individual country has an incentive to free-ride on the efforts of others. Without cooperation we, not the fish, will get fried.

Coordinated international responses are getting both more necessary and more difficult. It is tempting to diagnose past failures as being entirely attributable to the unilateral tendencies of the Bush administration and to expect the Obama administration to usher in an era of strong global governance: a reformed United Nations with new powers; a new global authority to assign internationally marketable rights to carbon emissions; and a new global regulatory authority for the financial system. I do not expect anything so dramatic. Simply look at the problems of the United Nations, for example. Reform of the Security Council has been blocked for decades by governments that do not want to see their regional rivals getting representation: Italy blocks Germany, Korea blocks Japan, and Indonesia blocks India. There is no new architecture for global governance that would satisfy China and yet enshrine principles of democracy. Although in the wake of Rwanda the UN managed to introduce a Responsibility to Protect that could overrule national sovereignty in certain extreme conditions, in practice the block vote of poorly governed states is sufficiently large to frustrate its implementation. The roots of the decline in cooperation between governments go deeper than recent events.

Yet while the ability of governments to cooperate has declined, the ability of citizens to coordinate action—as I've suggested by singling out Clay Shirky—has increased. The Obama campaign provides another spectacular demonstration of this. It may be that cooperation at the level of civil society can be a substitute for that between governments in introducing common responses to global problems. Were citizens around the world armed with shared and reliable information, their pressure, country-by-country, could be as effective as a top-down inter-government agreement.

The conventional, top-down approach led by international cooperation between governments is for a global assignment of rights to catch fish or to emit carbon, matched by the creation of a global market in which these rights can be traded between countries. In practice, there are many obstacles to reaching such a top-down agreement between governments. There simply is no nonarbitrary basis for assigning such valuable rights. If rights are based on historic emissions the rich world would hold them; if they are based on the threat of future emissions the emerging market economies would hold them; if they are based on poverty the bottom billion would hold them. International transfers resulting from these rights could easily dwarf aid flows and so be fought over. Governments would have a powerful incentive and considerable scope to game whatever incentives were offered. As those societies that were paying huge sums realized that what they were buying was often fraudulent, the willingness to pay would collapse.

The bottom-up approach of providing common information about the problem to ordinary citizens is already proving more effective than this top-down approach. With astonishing speed the sharing of information has changed the political landscape. First in Europe, and more recently in America, ordinary citizens have grasped what their societies need to do to limit carbon emissions. They have pressured their governments to impose a mixture of taxation and regulatory controls on emissions. European governments and now the Obama administration have adopted these proposals for national schemes. Changes in policy have followed, not led public awareness. So long as individual governments respond to pressures from their own citizens, formal international cooperation between governments becomes both less important and easier to achieve.

For any particular global problem, the approach that is most feasible therefore depends upon what citizens, country-by-country, conclude is acceptable. I have suggested that fish and carbon may be best suited to different approaches. The rights to international fish are relatively uncomplicated and are nowhere near as valuable as those to carbon. I have suggested letting the money accrue to the United Nations. This assumes that citizens do not regard their own country as having rights to the fish in international waters, and can readily understand that the plunder of unassigned ownership must be avoided. They are capable of thinking beyond their borders, and beyond their own lifetimes.

Such an approach would likely not work for carbon. Although a global liability, it is emitted country-by-country and the sums involved are going to be huge. I very much doubt that citizens would be content to see such huge transfers made to the United Nations, or for that matter to purchase somewhat dubious indulgences at vast expense from firms or governments in other countries. However, citizens around the world can surely accept that their country should not be guilty of free-riding on the efforts of others, or worse, of undermining those efforts. The same activity should have to pay the same amount for the carbon it emits wherever it is located. People everywhere can recognize that their society should not be the weak link in enforcement. However, the activity can make its payment to the government in which the activity occurs: there is no particular reason for these payments to be transferred from the citizens in one country to those in another. While different countries may have the same emissions per activity they may have different emissions per citizen. There is nothing wrong with that, and indeed, over time, that pattern will change as industry continues to relocate to the emerging market economies. The changing national pattern of carbon liabilities is analogous to the changing pattern of natural assets: over time, technology will makes some aspects of nature more valuable and others less.

Citizens around the world can rally round the principle of a common treatment of carbon emissions by activity rather than by country. As I discussed, some countries might use carbon taxes and others quantitative emissions standards for an activity. The important thing is that the tax and the standards be equivalent. Such variation in approach would not deter global compliance. On the other hand, setting lower standards or lighter taxes in some countries than in others would not be consistent: people can readily recognize that it would be unfair.

The key to addressing global problems lies with the exploitation of the new collective power. This bottom-up approach holds out greater promise than re-engineering inter-governmental cooperation and also eases inter-government efforts. Yet it places on citizens the responsibility to be well-informed. Were consensus built on collective delusion, it would be nonsense on stilts. In this book I have tried to show the dangers, as well as the promise, of citizen power. In the rich countries, flirtation with the illusory idylls of nature has reduced global food supply, and the first victims are the urban poor in the societies of the bottom billion. Power without responsibility, traditionally the prerogative of the harlot, has become the prerogative of the romantic. Citizen power must be founded on hard-headed principles of ethical economics, not on the dream of returning to Camelot.

The emerging market economies are now collectively too important for natural assets and liabilities to be managed without their cooperation. Even were the rich countries to reduce their carbon emissions to zero, unless these emerging countries restricted their carbon emissions the world would still fry. When the resource-extraction companies of the rich world behave decently, refusing to be complicit in the plunder of the bottom billion, responsibility passes to the companies within these countries. Increasingly, these companies have proven they have the power to undermine international standards. In December 2008 a coup in Guinea installed a young captain as president. The regime was not recognized by the African Union and was effectively boycotted by companies. The following September the regime shot dead 157 people gathered to protest at the lack of democracy. The very next month a Chinese consortium struck a $7 billion deal with the government for resource extraction: plunder writ large.

And so the societies of the emerging market economies can no longer take shelter behind the supposed culpability of the rich countries. As in the rich countries, they must hold their governments to account. In many of these societies, and most notably in China, citizens have little experience in doing so but are learning from the technology that now crosses international borders with ease. Only a tiny handful of truly paranoid governments, such as that of North Korea, are able to keep their citizens in the dark.

I have tried to show why the societies of the emerging market economies cannot rely upon the argument that they should be allowed to do what the rich countries once did. The analogy should be how the rights of fishermen changed once fish stocks dwindled to the point at which fishing rights became valuable. Prior to the emergence of those rents anyone was free to fish; once the rights become valuable that changed. The era of cheap natural abundance is over. We must now compose common rules for an era in which nature is valuable.

The question is not whether the citizens of China and other countries will have the power to discipline their governments; citizen power will be unstoppable. If people recognize a common responsibility for the custody of the natural world then governments will have to deliver it. But power is no better than its underlying rationale. Just as citizens in the rich countries have been misled into an enticing agenda of romanticism, sirens of various sorts will beckon the citizens of the emerging market economies. Those sirens are unlikely to be romantic environmentalism. They will be romantic nationalism. What looms ahead is a battle between the ethics of custody and the seductive sentiments of national self-interest. You, like me, will be in that battle: through your ears, and through your voice.

A Note on Sources

THERE IS AN ENORMOUS ACADEMIC LITERATURE on the themes covered in this book. On the political economy of natural assets I recommend the work of Professor Michael Ross; on climate change, the work of Professor Lord Nicholas Stern; and on the interactions between nature and development, the work of Professor Sir Partha Dasgupta.

My own current research is posted on my Web site: http://users.ox.ac.uk/~econpco.

By the author
"Laws and Codes for the 'Resource Curse,'" *Yale Human Rights and Development Law Journal* (2008) 11: 9–28.
"Principles of Resource Taxation for Low-income Countries," in Philip Daniels, Michael Keen, Charles McPherson et al., eds., *The Taxation of Petroleum and Minerals: Principles, Problems, and Practice*, Routledge, London, 2010.

With Lisa Chauvet
"Elections and Economic Policy in Developing Countries," *Economic Policy*, 24 (Issue 59): 509–550.

With Benedikt Goderis
"Structural Policies for Shock-prone Developing Countries," *Oxford Economic Papers* (October 2009) 61: 703–726.
"Does Aid Mitigate External Shocks?" *Review of Development Economics*, 13 (3): 429–451.
"Prospects for Commodity Exporters: Hunky Dory or Humpty Dumpty," *World Economics*, 8 (2): 1–15.
"Commodity Prices, Growth and the Natural Resource Curse: Reconciling a Conundrum," CSAE WP.

With Anke Hoeffler
"Testing the Neo-con Agenda: Democracy in Resource-rich Societies," *European Economic Review*, 53 (3): 293–308.
"Democracy's Achilles Heel: How to Win an Election without Really Trying," CSAE WPS 2009-8.

With John Page
Industrial Development Report 2009, *Breaking In and Moving Up: New Industrial Challenges for the Bottom Billion and the Middle-Income Countries,* 2009, United Nations Industrial Development Organization.

With Tony Venables
"Trade and Economic Performance: Does Africa's Fragmentation Matter?" In J. Lin and B. Pleskovic, eds., *Annual World Bank Conference on*

Development Economics 2009, Global: People, Politics, and Globalization, World Bank Publications, February 2010.

"Illusory Revenues: Tariffs in Resource-rich and Aid-rich Countries," CEPR Discussion Paper no. 6729. London, Centre for Economic Policy Research, 2009. Forthcoming in the *Journal of Development Economics.*

"International Rules for Trade in Natural Resources," *Journal of Globalization and Development* (2010) 1 (Issue 1): article 8.

With Tony Venables and Gordon Conway
"Climate Change and Africa," *Oxford Review of Economic Policy* (2008) 24: 337–353.

With Tony Venables, Rick van der Ploeg, and Mike Spence
"Managing Resource Revenues in Developing Countries," *IMF Staff Papers,* 2009.

Index

He just wanted a decent book to read ...

Not too much to ask, is it? It was in 1935 when Allen Lane, Managing Director of Bodley Head Publishers, stood on a platform at Exeter railway station looking for something good to read on his journey back to London. His choice was limited to popular magazines and poor-quality paperbacks – the same choice faced every day by the vast majority of readers, few of whom could afford hardbacks. Lane's disappointment and subsequent anger at the range of books generally available led him to found a company – and change the world.

'We believed in the existence in this country of a vast reading public for intelligent books at a low price, and staked everything on it'
Sir Allen Lane, 1902–1970, founder of Penguin Books

The quality paperback had arrived – and not just in bookshops. Lane was adamant that his Penguins should appear in chain stores and tobacconists, and should cost no more than a packet of cigarettes.

Reading habits (and cigarette prices) have changed since 1935, but Penguin still believes in publishing the best books for everybody to enjoy. We still believe that good design costs no more than bad design, and we still believe that quality books published passionately and responsibly make the world a better place.

So wherever you see the little bird – whether it's on a piece of prize-winning literary fiction or a celebrity autobiography, political tour de force or historical masterpiece, a serial-killer thriller, reference book, world classic or a piece of pure escapism – you can bet that it represents the very best that the genre has to offer.

Whatever you like to read – trust Penguin.